Discover Your PHENOMENAL DREAM LIFE

17 Principles to Reach Your Phenomenal Destiny

Howard Partridge

Copyright © 2023
Howard Partridge

Performance Publishing
McKinney, TX

All Worldwide Rights Reserved.
All rights reserved. No part of this publication may be reproduced, stored in a retrieval system or transmitted, in any form or by any means, electronic, mechanical, recorded, photocopied, or otherwise, without the prior written permission of the copyright owner, except by a reviewer who may quote brief passages in a review.

Paperback: 978-1-961781-24-5
eBook: 978-1-961781-23-8

CONTENTS

Acknowledgements 6

Foreword by Michelle Prince 7

Introduction 10
    Do You Have a Phenomenal Dream?

Chapter 1 33
    God is LOVE

Chapter 2 42
    You Are a Phenomenal Product

Chapter 3 46
    Dream Intentionally

Chapter 4 50
    Your Dreams Fuel Your Life

Chapter 5 55
    In Dreams and in Love there are No Impossibilities

Chapter 6 58
    The Dream Starts with You

Chapter 7 67
    Dreams DO Come True

Chapter 8 70
    Trust God. Love Others.

Chapter 9 74
    Vision Without Action is a Daydream

Chapter 10 80
    Go Confidently in the Direction of Your Dreams

Chapter 11 84
    Think and BE Phenomenal

Chapter 12 87
    Be Transformed by the Renewing of Your Mind

Chapter 13 90
    Pray Without Ceasing. Be Anxious for Nothing

Chapter 14 95
    I Can Do All Things Through Him Who Strengthens Me

Chapter 15 99
    Stay Humble

Chapter 16 102
    Live in Freedom Every day

Chapter 17 108
    My God Will Supply All Your Needs According to His Riches in Glory in Christ Jesus

Chapter 18 117
    See You At the Top

Conclusion 119
    "I Almost Quit"

To My Princess Denise

Thank you for standing beside me and cheering my dreams on. May we spend many years walking the dream beach together. I love you with all my heart.

—Your Knight in Shining Armor

ACKNOWLEDGEMENTS

Thank you Santiago, Michelle, Rick, Victoria, and Daena for believing in me, and literally helping me achieve my dream by being my phenomenal dream team! Your support, encouragement, and accountability have been invaluable.

Thank you Scott, Johann, and Aliki for doing a phenomenal job running the service company—the foundation for everything else.

Thank you Daena Ciomperlik for editing this book and challenging me to work harder on it. It is better because of you.

Thank you Laurie Magers for your "sign off" as my "best book yet."

Thank you Tom Ziglar for believing in me and giving me a platform to help others.

Thank you to all of our clients and members who support us financially, as well as emotionally and spiritually.

FOREWORD

I met Howard Partridge in 2010 at Ziglar headquarters while I was hosting Ziglar's Success 2.0 webcast and Howard was the guest. We immediately hit it off! We both have a love for Zig Ziglar and a dream to make a difference. You could say we are "2 P's in a POD" (more on that later).

Howard has been and continues to be a huge influence in my life. His enthusiasm for life, love for people, and dedication to serving others makes it an honor to write the foreword to a book that I KNOW will make an incredible impact on the lives of so many people...people like you who have a dream and are ready to reach for it!

Discover Your Phenomenal Dream Life will bring clarity to your dream and outline the steps you need to take to reach your biggest goals. The 17 principles that Howard shares will guide you through the process of discovery and show you exactly what you need to do to find your purpose and live your best life. My long-time mentor, Zig Ziglar, says, "You were designed for accomplishment, engineered for success, and endowed with the seeds of greatness." I love that quote because what it really means is that you have everything you need to be successful in life already within you! You were born with those "seeds" and God created

YOU for greatness! It's time to discover your phenomenal dream and let those seeds take root. Howard Partridge is just the guy to help you do it!

One of the things I love most about Howard is how alike we are in our thinking, our dreams and goals; especially when it comes to helping people find their purpose and live their best. In fact, our thoughts are so aligned that while Howard was writing this book and creating the "17 Principles to Find Your Purpose, Reach Your Biggest Goals and Fulfill Your Destiny," that he'll share with you in this book, I was also working on a similar project called *Michelle's PRINCE-iples of Success*, but neither of us knew what the other was doing. Ironically, not only did we both create principles to help people find their purpose, but our messages beautifully align and complement one another, so much so, Howard asked me to share them briefly with you.

It all starts with *Passion*. What lights you up? What do you love to do? Your passion is a clue to your *Purpose*. We all have a purpose. God created you for greatness, as you'll discover in this book, so finding your purpose is the key to living your best life. Once you know your purpose, and your reason for living, you'll have clarity on your *Priorities*. You'll know exactly what you need to be working on and what tasks need to be completed. Clarity on your priorities will ultimately lead you to better *Performance*. When you're successful in an area, and others take notice, that performance will allow you the privilege of building a *Platform*. This platform is the key to helping more people, but you don't get a platform by just wanting one; it only comes when you can prove your performance. But it's hard to perform if you don't know your priorities, and if you don't know your priorities then you likely don't know your purpose, and if you don't know your purpose then you probably have little to no passion. So, if passion leads to purpose, and purpose brings clarity to your priorities and your priorities allow you to have greater performance and your performance enables you to build a platform, then helping more people will lead to *Prosperity*. Prosperity can come in many different forms, but when you know that you're doing what you've been called to do, making a difference in other people's lives, and impacting the world, that's ultimately when you have *Peace*. The peace of knowing that one day you'll hear your Father say, "Well done, thou good and faithful servant."

I am certain that Howard Partridge will hear those words one day and I pray you will too! I am blessed to call Howard my friend. We encourage, challenge and mastermind with each other to push farther and reach higher. He calls this a POD™ (Power of Discovery) and, through this book, you'll get to experience that same mentorship from Howard too. So, now you know what I meant when I said that Howard and I are "2 P's in a POD!"

As you embark on this journey to find your purpose and all that comes with it, my wish is that you'll dream bigger, pray bigger, and know with all certainty that you have what it takes. Your dream is worth it…YOU are worth it!

Keep dreaming!

*** Michelle Prince***
Best-Selling Author, Zig Ziglar Speaker & Author Coach

INTRODUCTION

Do You Have a Phenomenal Dream?

Do you have a vision for your future that is so compelling and so exciting that you can't wait to pursue it? Do you wake up every day so enthusiastic to tackle the day because you have a dream that is so phenomenal, it pulls you out of bed every morning?

If you're like most people, the answer is no. Sadly, most people don't have a clear picture of where they want to go in life, but they would be quick to say they want their life to be better.

The first thing I would like to share with you in this book is that you are *supposed* to have a dream. You are here for a reason; a special purpose that was designed long before you arrived on Planet Earth. God created you for a reason, and He has a plan for your life.

You've probably heard that before.

But have you taken the time to figure out what that purpose is? And what it really means? *Now* is the time to find out. Author Mark Twain has remarked, "The two most important days in a person's life are the day they were born and the day they find out why." This book will help you get a clear vision for your life so you can get where you're supposed to go!

In the following chapters, I'll be taking you through 17 principles that have been meaningful to me. Principles that will help you have a more meaningful life—principles that will give you clues to your purpose, and help you find your dream.

WHAT *IS* A DREAM EXACTLY?

My good friend and leadership expert John C. Maxwell says, "A dream is an inspiring picture of the future that energizes your mind, will, and emotion, empowering you to do everything you can to achieve it." I like that definition. If you're going to wake up excited to get going every day, there must be an inspiring picture—a vision—that compels you and excites you.

Unfortunately, most people wake up every day without a clear vision of who they are, Whose they are, and what the meaning of life is. The result is that they just get through the day. They have good days and bad days.

My hero and American legend, the late Zig Ziglar, said, "If you don't think every day is a good day, try missing one!" Obviously, there are good and bad things that happen in life, but if we live our lives solely by circumstance, we'll be on an infinite roller coaster of emotion.

Sure, you're going to be happy when things are going well and you're going to be sad when things aren't going your way, but living life with a purpose—living life according to a meaningful vision rather than circumstances, will give you deep joy and fulfillment, and the inspiration to keep going, regardless of the circumstances.

Instead of having a goal to be comfortable, or "happy," have a goal to be *significant*. When you're making a difference in others' lives, you'll be filled with joy. I have a plaque on my desk that reads, "Success is making a difference in others' lives. Happiness is watching them grow because of it."

People may think that I'm joyful because of all the nice things I have and the life I get to enjoy, but the truth is, the reason I do what I do is because we change lives. The dream life I have is simply the result of following the principles in this book that anyone can practice.

I do what I do because of people like Alan and Debbie Hunter, who lost their only daughter when she was barely 21. She took a drug for the first time in her life, and it took her life. This "feel good" drug called Molly was laced with a deadly substance. Our community walked through that horror with them and supported them through it. Watching the love that flowed toward that couple was amazing.

To see how they have come through the ordeal with a vision and a purpose to help others avoid the same fate is inspiring. They started a non-profit (www.iknowjessica.com) that brings awareness about drug abuse to young people.

Alan speaks to schools and youth groups to spread the message. He and Debbie have a phenomenal attitude of gratitude. They are grateful for the time they had with Jessica, and they now have a specific purpose for their lives.

I do what I do because of people like Alyse Makarewicz. Our coaching community and what we teach helped her save her marriage.

I do what I do because of people like Brenda Sell. Senior Grandmaster Brenda J. Sell is the highest-ranking female in Tae Kwon Do in the world. She lost her husband to cancer and knew nothing about running their business, since he had handled all of that. Her mother, who handled the administration side of the business, fell ill and couldn't work. Then her father passed away as well. Practically left alone to run the business, Brenda herself was diagnosed with breast cancer. For two years, our coaching community walked with her through the ordeal. Not only did she survive, but her business did too.

Sure, my work has helped countless business owners add hundreds of thousands—even millions—of dollars to their bank accounts, and they've built dream homes and taken amazing vacations. Some of our coaching clients have gotten out of debt, bought and sold businesses, and done many other amazing things through our training and coaching, but I'm called to this work because of people like our client Ted Wilson.

Ted sent me an e-mail sharing how he had realized he had been approaching his life in entirely the wrong way. He wasn't the person he wanted to be. Through learning from us, his life began to change and he got his daughters involved. Attached to the e-mail were two handwritten book reports on my book, *Think and Be Phenomenal*, by his 13-year-old daughter, Bailey, and Brianna who was only 11. They are both printed here with permission:

"I am Phenomenal", is an everyday thought that should be applied to your life. Some people say you are what you eat, but after reading "The 5 Levels of Being Phenomenal" it should be, you are what you think.

Zig Ziglar said, "You are what you are and where you are because of what has gone into your mind. You can change what you are and where you are by changing what goes into your mind." By telling yourself you are phenomenal, I can do this, and nothing can stop me, is how you can change what goes into your mind. And change who you are.

Reading this book has helped me to understand that you can do anything as long you THINK you can and put your mind to it. Having confidence in yourself will help your performance and personality in everything you do. Weather it's telling yourself that you can reach a certain goal, or you can get an A on a test. And the 5 Levels of Being Phenomenal

—can help you do just that.
The first level to being Phenomenal is to have self-Awareness. You have to become aware of a new habit or skill you want in your life. Self Awareness allows you to focus on the truth. You can't move forward with your goals or life until you face reality. You have to decide on what you really want in life and don't let fear get in the way. If your goal is to become a forward on your soccer team, don't be scared because you've never done it before or you think your not fast enough. BE CONFIDENT

The Second Level is to have willingness to change. You have decide that the change in you, is actually what you want. Nobody likes change. For me, I'll set a goal. Go through with it for awhile. Get a little "busy". Then come up with excuse after excuse. Obviously I was not willing to change nor did I want to reach that goal enough. Keep pushing and pushing yourself

— and find some motivation to keep you going.

The third step is to have controlled attention. You have to be focused on doing things differently. This is where you turn your new idea or goal into a habit and it requires all your focus and attention. You have to focus on what you're doing and why your doing it.

The fourth step is to have commitment. This is the level where all your habits start to form. Zig said, "commitment helps you overcome obstacles." If you commit to practicing your soccer skills everyday, you would expect to get the forward position you were wanting. You plan to prepare to win.

The fifth level to becoming Phenomenal is character. Your values have truly changed. Your character is who you are, when your reputation and your values match, you are living a life of integrity.

> If you truly believe that you can reach a goal, you're bound to reach it.

And Brianna's report…

Being Phenomenal all starts by how I think of myself. Frank Outlaw said "When you change your THINKING, you change your BELIEFS when you change your beliefs, you change your EXPECTIONS when you change your expections you change your ATTITUDE when you change your Attitude you change your PREFORMANCE when you change your preformance you change your LIFE" he also said "Watch your THOUGHTS they become WORDS, watch your words the become ACTIONS, watch your actions the become your CHARACTER, watch your character they become your DESTINY." So Frank Outlaw is basicly telling me to think about what I do before we do it or we will regret it. Frank Outlaw is also telling me to change one thing about myself at a time so I can change my Attitude and my life.

Zig Ziglar said "You are WHAT you are and WHERE you are because of what has gone into your MIND. YOU can CHANGE what you are and where you are by changing what Goes into your MIND." Zig Ziglar is telling me we do what we do because our minds are telling us to. And We can change our Actions or also Attitudes by changing our thoughts. If I want to be very REMARKABLE and EXTRORDINAY I have to have control over my habits and emotions. I have to be focused, Inspired and I have to know what I want to do in life. This book is also teaching me to listen carefully and pay more attention more to what I'm doing to be very successful in life.

I need to think about who I am. What can I do to become successful in life and where I can go from being successful in life. I think being successful and having good behavior wise can get me a good education, then I can get a good job and good money and become very successful in my life. Howard Partridge said, "without an inspiring picture, your mind, will and emotion won't be energized and you won't be empowered to do everything you can do to achieve in which means you won't take action, which is the key to results." So I need to learn how to take action in what I'm doing so I wont get in trouble. And when I start something I need to finish it without giving up or letting go of what I wanted in life because if I do I will never get it back.

After getting an e-mail like that, I could die and go to heaven and life would have been worth living. My "why" is helping others understand who they are and Whose they are, so they can become the person they were created to be and do the things they are supposed to do in order to have the life they were created to have. And that is what this book is all about. It's to convince you that your phenomenal dream life is waiting to be discovered.

As you become the person you were created to be, you'll be empowered to do the things you need to do, so you can have the life you're supposed to have. Everyone wants their life to have meaning.

The key to a meaningful life is to have a specific vision. Zig Ziglar encouraged us to not be "wandering generalities" but instead to be "meaningful specifics." He also said that the secret ingredient of success is desire, and desire comes from a vision. If you want to have a different life, you need a new vision. And that vision must be energized with desire.

Personal development pioneer Earl Nightingale said, "Whatever is planted in your subconscious mind and nourished with emotion and repetition will eventually become a reality."

Thoughts are things. Psychologist Dr. Caroline Leaf in *Who Switched Off My Brain* reveals the physical thought pattern in our mind that looks like a tree. You can allow weeds to grow in your mind, or you can intentionally plant a garden of dreams in the nutrient-rich soil of your God-given imagination.

The Two Kinds of Dreams

My friend and small business expert Michael Gerber says there are two kinds of dreams: The *personal* dream and the *impersonal* dream.

The personal dream is the house on the beach, or the once-in-a-lifetime vacation. A personal dream might be having your perfect career. It is something that benefits you *personally*.

An *impersonal* dream is something that will make a difference in the lives of others. Michael says that real dreams should be so big that it isn't possible to actually achieve them. He says that the impossible dream launches a vision. A vision is something you can actually reach.

But an impossible dream is necessary because it gives you the inspiration to create a vision that *is* possible. Rudy Ruettiger, the real guy from the movie *RUDY*, told me that a dream is a fantasy. Rudy had a fantasy of playing football for Notre Dame. That turned into a vision, which became a reality.

Personal dreams are exciting because they give you confidence. Personal dreams are beneficial because you have to stretch and grow to reach them. I learned from Zig that it's not what you *get* when you reach your goals, it's who you *become*. I'm a different person today because of the goals I've pursued. And the wonderful thing is that pursuing my personal goals has benefitted many other people along the way.

The more personal dreams you reach, the more you will be willing to believe in impersonal dreams. Impersonal dreams are the ones that give us lasting inspiration. When you see a person's life being changed, like Ted Wilson's daughters, you can wake up with satisfaction that life is worth living. Impersonal dreams add meaning to your life. John Maxwell once commented, "Once you get a taste of significance, success will never satisfy."

My Personal Dream

In my book *Think and Be Phenomenal*, I shared the story about one of my biggest personal dreams. I've included the first part of the story that was in my previous book so that the rest of the story makes sense...

In 1997 I found my dream property—a gated community with only 14 home-sites right next to my favorite beach in the Destin area, 3 1/2 miles of unspoiled State Park beach. I've never seen more than a handful of people on that beach. The sand is sugar white with huge, magnificent sand dunes. The water is emerald green and crystal clear. It's truly paradise.

That beach is where I go to dream. For some strange reason, there's one specific spot on the beach where I seem to get the most "energy." When I discovered it, a single lot was $300K. At that time, we were just building our dream home in Houston and I had just launched Phenomenal Products. It felt like it was too much of a stretch. Over the next few years, the lots began to disappear and the prices began to soar. Before long, there was only ONE lot left! The homes were $3.5M minimum, which was way out of our range at the time.

My goal was to acquire the very last lot and to hold it until I was ready to build our next dream home. Unfortunately, by this time, the lot itself had gone up to $1.4M. Over a million dollars for a pile of sand! Yet I still dreamed and planned how I could acquire it. My thoughts were recorded in my journal. I was THINKING of ideas that would help me raise enough money for that lot.

I thought about it EVERY DAY.

I asked myself if investing that much money in a lot was too much and wondered if it would be "ungodly" to spend that much on a piece of land. I had many mixed feelings. After a while, I determined that if I was willing to work hard, continued to tithe and support the work of ministry, and continued to make a difference in others' lives it was okay. As long as it did not take from anyone else, I felt comfortable pursuing it.

But I still didn't have ideas big enough to acquire it. Looking back, that's not true. I just didn't THINK big enough. One of the "blessings" of the economic conditions from 2008 to 2011 (for me) was that the property values plummeted. The lot dropped to $633K, then to $533K. We became very serious about grabbing the very last lot in Stallworth.

I put in an offer for $410K. They countered at $490K, which I accepted. However, I only had three days to secure a letter of credit. We could have paid cash, but all of our investments were in 401k plans, annuities, and other assets that would cost huge penalties in order to cash out. This wasn't a problem, since our credit was really good and this property had been on the market for so long.

My Houston bankers didn't do Florida property, especially land, so I went to a Destin bank. The very first bank I went to assured me that financing the lot for me was not a problem; however, they were being bought out by another bank and all loan officers were in Atlanta for a meeting. "Not to worry," she assured me. Two weeks later, the real estate agent representing the property called to inform me that he had a cash buyer and that he had to take the other man's offer.

My dream property was gone.

I was stunned.

To add insult to injury, the letter of credit came from the banker the very next morning. I quickly forwarded it to the agent and pleaded that he deny the cash buyer and to accept my offer since I was first.

"It's too late," he said.

I was pretty bummed out that day. Did I miss it? Was it against God's permission? Was I totally off base? Over the years, I somehow thought I was "supposed" to have this property—I know that's weird, but that's how I felt.

After licking my wounds for a while, two amazing things happened. First, I've trained myself to be grateful for what I have. So, I began thanking God for the blessed life I have. I cannot complain, and I had an overwhelming sense of gratitude.

Zig Ziglar said, "Of all the attitudes one can acquire, the attitude of gratitude is by far the most important and life changing." He also said, "Failure is an event, not a person." And finally, he said, "It's not what you GET by accomplishing your goals, it's what you BECOME."

IMPORTANT LESSON: Be content with what you have, but never be satisfied with your personal growth. Always be grateful for what you have, but always strive to BEcome a better person every day. Remember, it's not about the house and it's not about the stuff. It's about stretching your faith and your imagination to give you the experiences you need to help others.

It's about BEcoming.

When it comes to goals, sometimes you win by reaching the goal and other times you learn a valuable lesson. You reached a goal of BEcoming a better person.

In the midst of this gratitude session, something amazing happened. I had a thought... "Wait, it's NOT OVER!"

Real estate deals go bad all the time. From the little experience owning a few properties and knowing many real estate investors, I knew the deal could go "south" even if it was cash.

Then, something even more amazing happened. I began to remember that I was "supposed" to have this property. It was mine!

That was my dream. The other guy was a real estate developer. He wanted the property just for the money. I'm sure he has dreams like everyone else, but his goal was a lucrative real estate deal.

My dream is to LIVE there with my phenomenal wife, to walk and pray on that beach, to THINK about how I can impact more lives and to DREAM about how I can do as much good during my one-time stop on this planet!

I'm risking being a little arrogant here; please stay with me.

Although I am GRATEFUL for what I have today, I am NOT going to let my dream slip away because of circumstances. God hasn't shut it down yet. A little circumstance called competition has gotten in the way. Am I just going to stand by and let someone take my dream away?

NO WAY!

So, I contacted the real estate agent (who is certain that I'm crazy at this point—I've called him just about every year for the last decade prior to this encounter). "Listen. I know this other guy supposedly has cash. But real estate deals go south all the time," I said, "I want to have my contract in play so that when this thing doesn't work out with him, we can move forward with our deal." At this point, I've gone from "if" the other deal doesn't work out to "when" it doesn't work out!

He responded, "Well, this guy has cash and buys a lot of properties... I'm sure there won't be a problem..." I insisted, "I know you probably think I'm crazy, but I've got a feeling he isn't going to come through... how many days does he have?" "Seven," he responded. "Okay, will you let me know the minute this deal doesn't work out with him? And please put my contract in play as the first back up so I don't lose this opportunity again. You know I've been working on this a long time."

I pressed. "Okay, I can do that, but I think it's a waste of time," he replied.

Every day after that I checked in with him by e-mail, text, or a phone call, and made sure that I dropped a seed of doubt (sounds bad doesn't it?) each and every time. I would say something like, "Just let me know when it doesn't work out. I'm ready!"

Now he knows I'm crazy!

Seven days come and go. "So what's the verdict?" I texted. " The owner gave him three more days," he replied. "Hmmm... what's the problem?" I asked. "He's requesting the homeowners association move a boundary on the property." That statement gave me more confidence than ever because I knew one thing... that AIN'T gonna happen! "Okay, I'll talk to you tomorrow." (I'm sure that made his day.)

Three days later I left him a voice mail. "Are you ready to do my deal? The other guy is out, right?" A text comes back. "I'm working on putting you in first and him in second." Two hours later, his assistant sent over the contract and we bought the property.

The lesson I learned was to be grateful, content, and patient, but to never give up if it's something you truly believe in, and if you're not 100% sure that God has shut the door. How would I have felt if I gave up and found out later that the deal with the "cash guy" went south and someone else got my dream property?

THE REST OF THE STALLWORTH STORY...

Acquiring the lot was just the beginning. When will we build a home there? How long will I sit on this property? Denise was contemplating retirement, so we bought a cute little house in Destin so that we would have something more spacious than our small condo.

Introduction

We put a substantial down payment on that house, and I began to work with an architect on the plans for Stallworth. After paying for that mortgage and the monthly payment on the Stallworth lot, I realized that I could finally obtain my dream home.

Once the plans were done, I began to shop for builders. I met Shane Babin at one of his job sites. "How are you?" I said as I shook his hand. "Phenomenal!" he responded. Impressed that he knew the right "word," I assumed he had done his research. "Oh, you must have read my book or been on my website." I responded. "No, why?" he said. "Okay, you're pulling my leg right?" I shot back. "Why did you choose to use the word *phenomenal?*" I pressed. "A friend of mine says that all the time," he said.

Hmmm… Could this be a sign? I liked Shane from the beginning, and more importantly, so did Denise. Without a doubt, we contracted him to build our dream home.

After the funding was finalized and he had the "go-ahead" to start, nothing happened. For over two months! When I inquired, he said, "The county won't give me a permit. I've been down there just about every day for weeks!" he said exasperated. "Why not?" I asked, taken aback. "There's some kind of new ordinance for coastal dune lake properties." Shane responded.

I got on the phone with my architect, Matt Savoie, who I had paid over $50K for plans at this point. Matt was easy to work with and had done several other homes in Stallworth. He's a straight shooter and a really easy going guy. "Yeah, it's a real problem, Howard. The county just came up with these new ordinances, and there are a lot of property owners in the same boat as you. In fact, they've formed a class-action lawsuit. I would recommend you get in on that."

"Are you kidding me?" I'm thinking to myself. "What are my options?" I asked my architect. "Well, according to the county, they are rendering the property unbuildable, because you don't have enough space to satisfy the small building footprint they are limiting you to."

I've never felt more stupid and more aggravated in my entire life. I have over $500K into this thing, and I've just gotten funding for another $900K and I'm hearing the word *unbuildable*? Incredible! The only good news the architect had for me was that they would be required to buy my property back from me, but wasn't certain how much they would pay or how long it would take.

I called the attorney that was handling the class-action suit. The only words I remember were that it would cost tens of thousands of dollars and would probably take several years. My neighbor pushed me to get on board.

One thing I've learned over the years is not to panic, but to pray. Especially when I sense that God is in something. Denise and I began to pray. I sensed that there was a way around the ruling. I pressed my architect and after a few days he sent me an e-mail and said, "I think I found something." "What is it?" I asked. "There's a different rule that may apply on your property depending on how they measure it," Matt said.

I happened to be in Destin and was planning a trip to the county offices with my builder the next day. "Can you draw it for me real quick?" "Sure, but remember, it depends on how they measure it," Matt cautioned me.

Denise and I prayed again before I went to meet Shane. I sweet-talked the ladies in the office and they got me in to see the man who would decide the fate of my new dream home on "my" dream beach.

I showed him the new drawing of the building footprint that Matt did. He got his calculator out and began punching numbers, squinting, frowning, and hitting the keys over and over. Shane and I were frozen with anticipation. Finally, the guy says, "I think this will work." *What did he just say?* I'm thinking to myself. "Is that a *yes*?" I finally had the guts to ask. "I think so. I'll have a signed copy for you at 3:00 today."

I walked out of that office into the parking lot with Shane. Both of us shaking our heads, bewildered by what had just happened. Why didn't anyone see this before? I have to believe that God just wants us to go through the struggle sometimes.

There was one more little (big) thing God did for me, that shouldn't be overlooked. The lot is in a special flood zone that does not qualify for regular flood insurance. My neighbor told me that his flood insurance was going to be $40K per year, so he decided to self-fund it. We designed the home with that in mind, but as I began to look at the line that represented the flood zone, it didn't come near the house on the plans. I later learned that this was the boundary the "cash buyer" was trying to get changed—and the reason he backed out.

I asked my architect how to get an exception on this issue since the boundary didn't come near the building envelope. He gave me numbers for the local fish and wildlife services. After multiple phone calls, I learned that the only office that could make the declaration for me was the U.S. Fish and Wildlife Services in Washington, D.C., and I was told that it would take *years* if I could ever get them to respond.

It took 21 days and I had a sealed document in my file.

Shane Babin has done a phenomenal job building our new

dream home on the dream beach, and by the time you read this book, we will be living there. I don't know why God has been so gracious to us, but I hope that He is even more so to you.

MY IMPERSONAL DREAM

Several years ago, I attended Michael Gerber's *Dreaming Room* experience. There were about 30 attendees in the room. There was a large artist's pad on the table in front of each one of us, with a bundle of different colored Sharpies held together by a rubber band. Michael walked in the room wearing a white suit and a pink tie and talked for a few minutes about having a "blank piece of paper and a beginner's mind," and then walked out of the room.

I expected that someone else would come to the front of the room, but no one did. The participants looked at each other not really knowing what to do except draw our dream. DRAW? I began to wonder if attending this event was a mistake. Some people went to work right away, and others just sat there with a stare as blank as the paper in front of them.

Finally, I began to draw circles with the letters "IC" inside of them, which stood for our "Inner Circle PODS." Then there was a beach (of course), and before I was done, there were statements that talked about Living in Freedom Every day and about building community.

That weekend I created my Dream, my Vision, my Purpose, and my Mission as Michael teaches us to do in his phenomenal book *Awaken The Entrepreneur Within*.

What was that dream? My Dream is for small business owners

to experience community. My Vision is 200 cities that have 50 small business members in each location that are experiencing community together. My Mission is to create community in every enterprise I create. And My Purpose is to help people have more L.I.F.E.

In my first book, *7 Secrets of a Phenomenal L.I.F.E.*, I share that L.I.F.E. stands for Living In Freedom Everyday. What I mean by that is you can be free in your mind and in your heart. You can know who you are and Whose you are. You can think and you can love. No matter what happens *to* you, you can *choose* how you'll respond.

So, are you ready to discover your phenomenal dream life so you can reach your phenomenal destiny?

CHAPTER 1

GOD IS LOVE

As I mentioned in the opening, there is no doubt that you have a purpose because God made you. Why would God create you and put you here with no purpose and no plan?

He wouldn't.

Although it may not be your time to find the *specific* purpose God has for your individual life, you can live out the fulfilling purpose God has for *every* life. You can have meaning and fulfillment in your life right now.

Here's how, and here's why...

Let's start with the premise that God created you. Why? The best-selling book *Purpose Driven Life* by pastor Rick Warren begins with this statement:

"It's not about you." "Well, if it isn't about me, who in the world is this life all about?"

It's about God.

God created you to be His child. He created you for the same reason that humans have children—to love you, cherish you, and have a relationship with you. He created you to reflect His love to others.

The difference between God and man, however, is that God is holy and we are not. Because He is holy and He is our maker, we worship Him in a way that we do not worship our earthly fathers.

With this truth as our foundation, the first step to your phenomenal dream is to come to know God, to have a relationship with your Father in Heaven. If you don't take that first step, you'll be on your own to find your dream. I don't know about you, but if God is real, I want to know who He is, and I want His input in my life. I want to know *His* dream for my life.

So, who is God? It's no secret that I am a believer in Jesus Christ. And the New Testament teaches us that God is Love. The problem is that even when we think we know who God is, we often don't know how to define love.

One time I sent my protégé Santiago to a training and he came back with this exercise:

When you're in a group of people, ask each person to write down five words that describe love. You'll be shocked at how few have the same definitions. But God has not left us to interpret.

His word for love comes from a Greek word called *agape*, which means unconditional. God is Love, means that He loves you unconditionally. No matter what. It doesn't matter what you've done in the past. It doesn't matter what you did yesterday. The Scripture says, "While we were yet sinners, Christ died for us."

I'm not going to get into the "gospel" right now. The point is that if God is real, and He made you, and He wants to have a relationship with you, there's no way to avoid the first step and reach your God-given purpose and destiny in life.

The Purpose Formula

Over the past few years of coaching people and learning from some of the world's top authors on leadership and personal development, I've identified some clues to helping people find their purpose in life.

In his book *Intentional Living—Choosing a Life that Matters*, John Maxwell suggests we ask ourselves three questions that will give us some clues about our purpose:

1. What do you cry about?
2. What do you sing about?
3. What do you dream about?

A few years ago, I became a certified trainer in *The One Thing* by Gary Keller. In that training, there's a purpose exercise that asks these two questions:

1. What are five things you would do for free?
2. What are five problems you would solve if you could?

When you match your passion with a problem you want solved in the world, you have a strong clue about your purpose.

Dave Ramsey is a great example of this. The problem he wants solved is the problem of *debt*. What would he do for free? *Teach*. In fact, he began teaching this subject in Sunday school before he ever got paid for it.

Last year I was with Dave as he was filming his part in the documentary film *Zig—You Were Born To Win*, that Dave and I are both featured in. He shared how his "overnight" success happened over a twenty-five year period of broadcasting on radio stations in little towns that had few listeners. He recounted the trials and tribulations he endured throughout his career. If Dave

Ramsey weren't passionate about solving the problem of debt, he would not have endured.

In his book *Better than Good*, Zig Ziglar said, "The place where your deep gladness meets the world's needs is where you'll find your purpose."

Remember to allow God to lead you there. Make sure your dream and your purpose are God-driven.

THE PURPOSE TRIANGLE

Here's a diagram that will help you visualize your path.

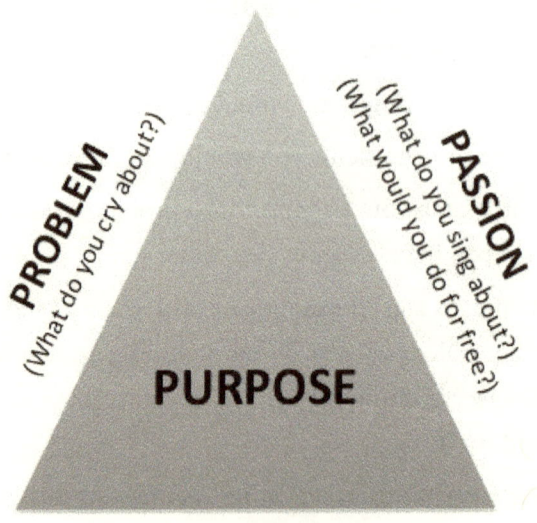

Every person has a unique gift, just like they have a unique fingerprint.

You have potential because you were created. The journey begins with finding your gift. What are you good at? What do people tell you you're good at? If you don't know, ask those that are close to you. I hope you have a mentor, a coach, or a community of people close to you that can speak this truth into your life.

If you don't, start there. Start with assembling a community of people around you that can help you discover who you are. I'm so grateful for the many people in my life that support me, encourage me, and hold me accountable to become the person I was created to be.

One day, my coach Rick Jones was interviewing me on stage at one of our conferences. Rick was digging deep to try and find out what made me who I am. As he began to probe, he asked me why my early mentor Bill Beckham was so special to me. As the tears began to well up, I said, "He helped me see my gift."

Everyone needs someone like that in his or her life. Now Rick is that person for me. He is like a father to me. Chris Hogan, one of Dave Ramsey's celebrity speakers, shares that every person needs four people in their life: A coach, a mentor, a cheerleader, and a friend. We need community around us to help us find our gifts.

Next, look at the left side of the triangle. PROBLEM represents what you cry about. This is the unique problem you want to solve in the world. Dave Ramsey is solving a *debt* problem. John Maxwell is solving a *leadership* problem. Zig Ziglar solved a *self-image* problem.

Next is PASSION. What do you sing about? What would you do for free? For Dave, John, and Zig, it was to teach. That is true for me as well. I'm a teacher at heart, and I would teach people about dreams, small-business growth, and personal development, regardless of whether I got paid for it or not. The fact that I get paid to teach simply helps me reach more people.

The good news is you don't have to be a speaker, teacher, coach, consultant, or business owner. You can help people, and you can encourage others at any and every post in life. You just have to exercise your gift.

What do YOU like to do? What is your passion? To serve? To help? To write? To organize? Again, get your support community involved to help you recognize what you talk about all the time. That's a clue.

THE PATH

Once you discover your POTENTIAL (by finding your gift), the PROBLEM you want to solve, and your PASSION, you begin to find your PURPOSE. Now you need a PATH.

The path is a specific way to serve—it's something you can do to begin to solve the problem and to exercise your gift doing what you love to do. Isn't this sounding phenomenal already?

Your path is your mission. At Ziglar Legacy Certification, they press the attendees to find their personal mission. I enrolled one of my employees, Daena, because I saw that she had incredible gifts for speaking and teaching, and I wanted to develop her for the future. Obviously, being only 18, she didn't really know her purpose.

I woke up one morning with a Word from God to "help" more people. Zig's quote, "You can have everything in life you want, if you will just help enough other people get what they want," was burning in my mind. I felt I needed to make that my 2017 business plan—to help as many people as possible.

When I got out of bed, I saw that I had a text message from Daena that read, "I found my mission statement! To help today's youth find their path in a confusing world." I was overjoyed because another dream I have is to create a program that will help our youth, and I could slowly see that path forming.

Your path may be volunteering, blogging, or helping someone who is already working in that space. I was meeting another one of my precious team members named Deena. I hired Daena and Deena on the same day for two different companies. Weird I know, but that's how my strange life runs.

Over lunch, I shared the Purpose Triangle with Deena. The problem she wants solved is child abuse. What is she passionate about doing? Serving. So, I simply suggested that she begin to volunteer and serve at an organization that helps kids who have been abused. This will bring great meaning and purpose to her life. And who knows where Deena or Daena will end up as they pursue their respective paths.

It might be starting a business. That's what happened to me. I had a great business already, but I got bored with the business I was in. I loved what it did for clients, and I love my team, but I just didn't like doing any part of that business any longer.

I wanted to help small business owners have what I had—a great business with a team of people that experienced a sense of community, and clients who loved our service.

On a dark stretch of Texas highway heading to South Padre Island for the weekend at the beach with one of my buddies, we began to talk and dream. The seed for Phenomenal Products was born that night.

Chapter 1

Looking back now, my business wasn't ready for me to leave, but I may not have known that unless I started Phenomenal Products. I wrote a few manuals, and I began to do seminars. I started down a path I really knew nothing about. Little by little, I could see more of the path in front of me. I made many mistakes along the way, but today I live the dream life I'm writing to you about.

I'm living my personal dream and my impersonal dream because I first found my POTENTIAL. And I only found my gifts through mentors. Everyone has gifts. You have a gift, and you will find it most surely by creating a loving support community around you like Daena had at the Ziglar Legacy Certification.

I then found the PROBLEM I wanted to solve. I saw that business owners didn't have any freedom. I wanted to solve a life problem.

What is my PASSION? Teaching. I love to teach business growth and personal development. As I matched those two up, my PURPOSE emerged.

One special note about this: even when you find your path like I did, the road may not be abundantly clear. I spent many years on the path called Phenomenal Products before I clearly understood how to drive it. I had to learn more about myself and how to build that business in a way that was authentic to me.

Just because you find your PATH doesn't mean you've arrived. It means that your journey toward your dream is just beginning.

Understand that you have POTENTIAL.

Recognize the PROBLEM you want to solve.

Feel the PASSION you have.

Discover your PURPOSE.

Choose a PATH.

Don't worry whether it's the perfect path. It rarely is. You discover your true path by starting on *a* path. You don't have to be great to start, but you do have to start to be great. And you do want to be great, because God made you to be great! In fact, He made you phenomenal! As you go along, you'll discover more about yourself and eventually reach your destiny, which is living out your purpose and becoming the person you were created to be.

CHAPTER 2

YOU ARE A PHENOMENAL PRODUCT

WHEN I NAMED my company Phenomenal Products, I had no idea how important that name would become. At the time, I produced manuals and audio programs. The product was the material.

My early mentor Bill Beckham, the wisest man I know, spoke at one of my conferences and shared with the audience that *they* are the phenomenal product.

Zig Ziglar said that you were born to win. He said man is designed for accomplishment, engineered for success, and endowed with the seeds of greatness. You *are* a phenomenal product.

Everything God creates is phenomenal, and that includes you! In fact, man is made in God's image. We were made different from animals. Humans are unique. We have a mind. We have the capacity to create.

We have the ability to dream.

In fact, we were made to dream.

The problem is we don't know who we are! Most humans

suffer from a poor self-image. The result is that we fall into one of two ditches—the ditch of guilt, or the ditch of pride. A poor self-image manifests in all kinds of ways.

The ironic thing about humans is that on one hand we are created to be phenomenal, to do phenomenal things and to have a phenomenal life, but at the same time, we are messed up! Humans do weird things.

One challenge I have when I say that all humans are phenomenal is the fact that people do bad things. Scripture teaches that we are sinners. But when we come to know Christ, we are saints. In my book *Think and Be Phenomenal*, I share 73 Scriptures that identify who we are in Christ. If you know Him, you can claim that identity. That is your *position* in Christ. We must live out of our *position*, rather than our *condition*.

What if you don't know Christ? God loves you. Just like a loving parent, He wants to have a relationship with you. Have you ever thought about why God made you to begin with?

God made us to live with Him eternally. To have fellowship with Him. He created humans for the same reason people have children. To love them, and for them to love Him. But as you may know, sin came into the picture when the first humans, Adam and Eve, sinned. Therefore, everyone born after them inherited "original sin," which means we *inherited* that *condition*.

In much the same way, we arrive into this world as sinners. But we were created to be with our heavenly Father. We were born separated from Him because He is holy and we are not. Mankind has tried all kinds of ways to get back to God. Do good. Go to church, help others, pray, etc. But the Word of God says none of it is good enough.

But God had a plan all along. You've probably heard this Scripture: "For God so loved the world that He gave His only begotten Son so that whoever believes in Him will not perish, but have everlasting life." When you accept Jesus Christ as your Lord and Savior, you are reconciled to God and you're immediately forgiven of your sin (that you inherited), and rather than being on a track toward spiritual death and hell, you are filled with God's Holy Spirit, and you become a new creature in Christ.

I know this might be a lot to take in if you've never heard any of this, and it may even be surprising to find something like this in Chapter 2 of a book about dreaming, but if you read the last chapter of my book *7 Secrets of a Phenomenal L.I.F.E.* and the last chapter of *Think and Be Phenomenal*, you'll understand why I believe this with all my heart.

Someone else may be able to tell you how to find your dream, your passion, and your purpose without all of this "God and Jesus talk," but I cannot. It is who I am. It's all one package. In this book, you'll learn how I have been influenced and how I dream. I cannot speak for anyone else and I also want to point out that although I have faith in God, I am a flawed man in the flesh.

We all are. When you get to know me, you'll see how my dreams have been shaped by God's influence in my life.

The point is that all of us were created to be phenomenal, but to have a phenomenal life here on earth, and to have everlasting life, we need God to live inside of us.

So, are we sinners? Or are we saints?

In the flesh, we are desperate sinners, sold out to fear and fantasy. But with God's Spirit inside of us, we can live by faith and enjoy the freedom that comes with allowing God to live through us. After all, if we confess that God created us, and we believe that He loves us, why not allow HIM to lead our lives?

Every human being is a child of God. Every human being was created to be phenomenal. They just don't know it. What we think about ourselves will have a big impact on whether we pursue our dreams or not.

I'll talk a lot about thinking in this book. The first step is to think about God and who He is. He is phenomenal.

The second step is to think about you and who you are. You were created to be phenomenal, to do phenomenal things, and to have a phenomenal life.

CHAPTER 3

Dream Intentionally

THE KEY TO EFFECTIVE dreaming is being intentional about dreaming. In other words, dreams don't come true by themselves. They may seem to come into your mind on their own, but you must intentionally pursue those dreams for them to become a reality in your life.

Success doesn't happen by accident. It happens by *design*. Intentional Dreaming means taking time to get in a creative, relaxed, inspirational environment to *think*, pray, and dream. For me, it's the beach. This is one of the reasons I love Stallworth so much. It's next to my dream beach, which is the place I get more inspiration and more "spiritual downloads" than any place on earth.

To finish my second book, *The 5 Secrets of a Phenomenal Business*, I spent four days on The Great Barrier Reef. I was in Australia doing business training for the Ziglar Corporation and The Great Barrier Reef was on my "bucket list." So I tacked on a few days there, knowing it would be an inspirational place to write, and it was.

There I followed my normal intentional dreaming routine: I get up early and write for a couple of hours, and then I go out to the beach. After a swim, I sit down with a spiral notebook and begin to dream. There are no limitations; you simply allow your mind to drift. This is called "free association." Your mind begins with an idea and that idea leads to another idea and your mind associates one thought to the next.

When your mind is free to associate, your subconscious mind begins working on the problem or idea for you. This is the reason solutions come to you in the shower or when you wake up. Your mind has been free to drift and your subconscious mind is working out solutions.

Simply visualize your life with no limitations. Zig Ziglar called this a Dream List, which we will talk about later. Write down everything you want to BE, DO, or HAVE. Don't allow any negative thinking. Don't worry about not having enough money or that it is too big of a dream. Let it flow!

You can do more than you think you can, but when you intentionally *think*, you discover how much more you can do!

James Allen said in his book *As A Man Thinketh*, "Dream lofty dreams, and as you dream, so shall you become... the greatest achievement was at first and for a time a dream. The oak sleeps in the acorn; the bird waits in the egg.... Dreams are the seedlings of realities." Make a decision today to invest in Intentional Dreaming every day.

Having a turnkey business is a result of spending a lot of time thinking, dreaming, and praying. Stallworth is a result of investing a lot of time, thinking, dreaming, and praying. Inspiring people around the world today is a result of spending a lot of time thinking, dreaming, and praying.

Intentional Dreaming means carving out a specific time and

a specific place to think and dream. You have to plan the time. Several years ago, I began taking one day off a week. The day happens to be Sunday, and I don't do anything related to work at all. I don't make business appointments, I don't write, I don't do e-mail, and I don't even read anything related to business.

Having this time every week to simply allow everything that you've sown to blossom is a powerful experience that I highly recommend, and it can also be a powerful time to dream.

The rule I make for myself on my rest day is that I can't write anything down. I found that if I do, I automatically default into planning business stuff, so I just think, dream, and pray. Many of my best ideas come on Sundays, and I have to train myself to remember them. The power of *Sabbath Thinking* is that it forces you to go over and over the thought until it's embedded in your mind.

A few weeks ago, I was on the Stallworth Beach on a Sunday, and I decided to think through my life a year ago and compare it to where I am today. Then I thought through where I want to be one year from today. I used the seven core areas of life as my thinking process: Spiritual, Mental, Physical, Family, Career, Financial, and Personal.

Pacing back and forth on the beach, I thought about each and every area specifically. Where was I last year? Then, using the same process, going through each and every one, I thought about how I wanted each area to be different one year from today.

Of course I've already done this on paper, but taking the time to intentionally embed and plant it in my mind helps to seal it in my subconscious mind.

If you want to reach your biggest dreams in life, you must be intentional about it. Find an inspirational place where you can think, dream, pray, and pick out a subject to think about.

Many times when I'm on a long drive in the car, I will pick out a subject to think about. It might be a goal, a dream, a project I want to work on, or it might be a challenge I have. It could be business or personal, but I will go over all of the issues in my mind over and over to maximize the time.

Self-talk coaching is helpful in this scenario as well. I think that's one thing I love about my dream beach. I can sing and shout and no one is around to notice. There's something therapeutic about digging your feet and hands into the soft, cool sand and sprinkling the sand about. The other day I found myself doing a "snow angel" in the sand. I laughed out loud.

I encourage you to find an inspirational place where you can think without any distractions and think about your life. Think about your future. Get a vision for your life. Go to that place on a regular basis.

Once you've created a dream or vision for your life that is compelling and exciting to you, you'll have something to go back to.

When you have a problem, or a difficulty, or you just get depressed for no apparent reason, or when you feel tired, go back to your vision. And go back to your dreaming place.

Now, let's find out how to get that picture…

CHAPTER 4

Your Dreams Fuel Your Life

Zig said the secret ingredient to success is desire. And where does desire come from? It comes from a *vision*. Most people don't have a vision for their life; therefore, they don't have the inspiration needed to give them the energy to see their dream, much less pursue it.

The reason there is no vision? No belief.

People who don't have a dream simply haven't allowed themselves to see the vision. Recently, I had lunch with one of our coaching members and I asked him about his dream. "I have a problem dreaming," he said. By the way, this is very common. I took Roger through a simple exercise that went like this:

"Describe your perfect life five years from now." Roger began to share all about his lifestyle. The house, the car, what the kids were doing, what he and his wife were doing, how his work life was different, etc. After he spent a few minutes sharing the vision, I simply responded with "there's your dream."

"But I don't know how to get there!" he shot back. Boom. There's the problem. We get caught up in the HOW instead of the WHAT. I shared with Roger that it isn't important to know *how* right now. What's important is to simply place the vision in your mind for now. The only thing that matters is that it's a dream that gets you excited. And, of course, a dream that is fair to your family.

Once you get the picture, look at it every day and maybe several times a day. Personal development pioneer Earl Nightingale said, "Whatever we plant in our subconscious mind and nurture with repetition and emotion, will eventually become a reality."

First, get the *picture*. Don't worry about how right now. Please trust me on this. I can tell you from personal experience how many of my dreams—personal and impersonal—have come through because of this. For example, I saw my company in my mind before it was a reality. I saw myself living in my dream home before I even bought the property. Zig taught us that before you reach the goal, you have to see it in your mind first.

And if you happen to be a believer in Jesus Christ, consider what Jesus Himself said:

Therefore, I say to you, all things you pray and ask, believe that you have received them, and they will be granted to you. —Mark 11:24

It may take you a while to believe you can receive your dream; therefore, it's necessary to trust the process. Dreaming is a process. The important thing is that the picture compels you. Make sure the dream is so meaningful to you that it evokes emotion. If you don't feel excited about the picture you've created, you won't take massive action toward it.

You see, your dreams fuel your life. If you don't have a phenomenal dream, you won't have the inspiration to pursue it. A phenomenal dream gives you the fuel—the energy to pursue it.

You'll learn as we go that you can accomplish more than you ever thought you could. And if you allow God to have His way in your life, this Scripture will be helpful to you:

Chapter 4

Now to Him who is able to do far more abundantly beyond all that we ask or think, according to the power that works within us, to Him be the glory in the church and in Christ Jesus to all generations forever and ever. Amen. —Ephesians 3:20, 21

I've seen this come true in my life. I'm a big dreamer, and I can come up with some "whoppers," but I can say with all sincerity that I never could have imagined I would live the life I live today.

This principle is about understanding the importance of having an inspiring picture of the future that energizes your mind, will, and emotion that will empower you to do all you can to achieve it.

If you wouldn't crawl across broken glass to achieve your dream (or receive it as I like to say), then it isn't meaningful enough. Meaning gives energy. Purpose gives power. You may not know what your specific purpose is yet, or what the impersonal dream is, and God may not want you to know yet, so here's how to find your personal dream...

How to Find Your Dream

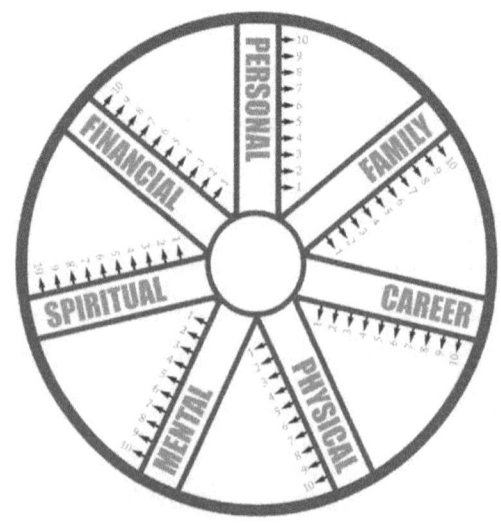

There's a phenomenal tool I love to use called The Wheel of Life. It has seven spokes on it: Spiritual, Mental, Physical, Family, Career, Financial, and Personal. I like to ask people which one of those areas they are supposed to be *UNsuccessful* in. They say "none," of course.

Our phenomenal God didn't create you to be mediocre in any area of life. Would you agree that if you rated the "spokes" of your life on a scale of 1-10, and you were a "border-line 11" on each spoke (as much as it depends on you, not others), that you would be living your dream life?

Of course you would!

Think about it. If you were being the person you know you need to be spiritually—you had the Peace of God, you were learning the things you needed to know, your thought life was pure, and you were in the best physical shape you could be in—you were being the spouse, father, mother, brother, or sister you know you should be—you were doing the work you were called to do—you made enough money to fulfill the vision you have for your life, and you were responsible with what God has entrusted you with—and you were doing what you want to do personally, would you be living a PHENOMENAL DREAM LIFE?

Of course you would! See how easy that was? If you simply create a picture of those seven spokes of your life, and you believe that you can win in each and every area of life, you would (should) be totally inspired!

Zig said you're born to win, but in order to be the winner you were born to be, you must plan to win and prepare to win before you can expect to win. When you plan to win and you prepare to win, you can expect to win.

Planning and preparing are key. Expecting is key. We will talk about this a little later in the book.

For now, do the Wheel of Life Assessment at http://www.howardpartridge.com/success

In this book, I'll take you through several dreaming exercises to give you the inspiration to implement the things you need to do for your phenomenal dream life.

CHAPTER 5

IN DREAMS AND IN LOVE THERE ARE NO IMPOSSIBILITIES

I WAS LEADING OUR LIVE weekly webcast and my good friend and colleague Ellen Rohr was my guest. We were talking about goals and she blurted out, "My goal is to visit all fifty states in the U.S." "How many have you been to?" I asked. "49," said Ellen. "Which one have you not been to?" I replied. "Hawaii," she said. "Well, we'll have to fix that."

Right then and there I told Ellen I was going to figure out how to get her to Hawaii. "HOW?" she asked, obviously shocked that I would just make that decision that quickly.

What Ellen didn't know is that I've been to Hawaii many times, and the last two times I went, I got paid to go. Ellen's experience building companies is so valuable that I knew I could get a few people together that would love to go to Hawaii to learn from Ellen and me. And that's exactly what we did. To top it off, I took two of my team members, and it was a trip of a lifetime for them.

During the Hawaii Master Mind, we had each person share a quote. Someone said, "In dreams and in love, there are no impossibilities." I love that. What that means to me is that if you can dream it, and God (who *is* Love) is with you, there are no limits.

Chapter 5

Nothing is impossible with God, and God uses people. Jim Rohn said, "You'll be changed most in life by the books you read and the people you meet." And, of course, the books you read are written by people, so in a way, you're meeting them.

I like to say it this way… "All of business and all of life is about relationships." Zig said, "You can have everything in life you want, if you will just help enough other people get what they want." We were created to belong to one another. We were made for community.

We must surround ourselves with people that will support us, encourage us, and hold us accountable to become the person we were created to be. And we must be willing to support, encourage, and help others be accountable. That's community.

We all have a longing for belonging. We need one another. I'm convinced that God created us with a people-shaped void just like we have a God-shaped void in our lives. The problem is we have allowed too many toxic people in our lives that have stinkin' thinkin' and need a check-up-from-the-neck-up!

You must be wise about who you spend time with. If you want to have a phenomenal dream life, you need a phenomenal dream team. Who do you have around you that is helping you with resources, ideas, and information? Who do you have around you that is encouraging you, constantly reminding you of what you are capable of? And who do you have around you that you can share your deepest concerns and failures with? Sadly, most people would say "no one."

Today, many people may reach material goals and accumulate wealth, but remain empty inside. We need faithful friends around us that we can count on. In order for that to be a reality, we must be that for others.

Who are you helping? Who are you encouraging? Who are you helping to be accountable?

You need a phenomenal dream team. I'm so grateful for my phenomenal wife, my phenomenal team, and the countless mentors, coaches, consultants, clients, members, and faithful friends that pray for me, pray with me, support me, encourage me, listen to me, cry with me, laugh with me, and truly have my best interest at heart. I must be that for them in order to receive it from them. And you must do the same.

Leadership expert Dave Anderson said, "If you have a dream, but no team, you've got to give up the dream or build up the team." I don't know about you, but I would hate to live my life knowing I never pursued my dream—both personal and impersonal.

It's sometimes hard getting close to people. The closer you get, the more likely it is that you'll get hurt. The old saying that "love hurts" is a true statement. But it's required for growth. If you aren't failing, you're not trying.

If you don't care about others, there won't be any meaningful emotions. I would rather live with the pain that comes from loving others passionately and getting close to them, than to live with the pain of emptiness that comes from keeping my guard up.

Building winning relationships is the most important life skill you can have. Your phenomenal DREAM TEAM will help you have your phenomenal DREAM LIFE. And, by the way, teamwork may make the dream work, but dream work makes the team work.

Make a commitment to help others, to encourage others, and that will lead to having a group of faithful friends that will help you become the person you were created to be.

CHAPTER 6

THE DREAM STARTS WITH YOU

Zig said, "You are what you are and where you are because of what has gone into your mind. You can change what you are and where you are by changing what goes into your mind."

What are you putting into your mind each day?

I love what Frank Outlaw said:

When you change your thinking, you change your beliefs.

When you change your beliefs, you change your expectations.

When you change your expectations, you change your attitude.

When you change your attitude, you change your behavior.

When you change your behavior, you change your performance.

When you change your performance, you change your life.

If you want to have a different future, you must change your thoughts.

Psychologist Dr. Caroline Leaf reveals that thoughts actually grow like plants. She shows how thoughts create energy and patterns in the brain and they look like bushes or trees. This is literally what happens when you focus on a certain thought over and over. Therefore, you want to be careful about what you think about and what you allow your mind to dwell on. You might end up with a lot of weeds in your garden!

So, your dream starts with you and what you think about. Most people, like Roger I mentioned earlier, won't allow themselves to dream because they don't know how. The dream begins in your mind. You have to conceive it before you can achieve it.

7 Ways to Dream

1. Pray. Since God made you and He has a purpose for your life, wouldn't it make sense to pray about your future? To ask God to show you His dream for your life? Pray that God would give you a vision. Pray that He would give you direction and wisdom. Pray that His will be done in your life.

Every day I pray in the morning that God would give me wisdom and that He would help me help other people. I pray for my family, my team, and a number of people God has put in my heart.

Then, throughout the day, I'm constantly lifting up prayers to God. Remember, He is always there as your Heavenly Father, so you can talk to Him anytime.

2. The Affirmation Statement. An affirmation is a statement of being set in the future. In others words, you speak of the future as if it were the present.

Here's mine for the summer of 2017: *"I am living at Stallworth full time. Denise has retired. My new book just became a #1 New York Times Best Seller. I am healthy and strong. My companies are hitting profits higher than anyone ever imagined. Our work is helping millions of people around the world…"*

This was written in 2016, and most of it is happening, and the rest is on the way. Each year, you'll "up" your affirmation a bit.

3. The Dream List or "Bucket List." One of the first things in the Ziglar Planner is the Dream List. You simply write a list of everything you want to be, do, or have with no limitations. Again, don't worry about how right now. Just write! Just dream!

My 2017 Dream List...

» Be a #1 *New York Times* Best Selling Author, world famous speaker, and influencer that makes dreams come true for as many people as possible.
» Own a sailboat in the Caribbean.
» Be the most loving, compassionate, joyful person anyone knows.

After you create your list, you then transfer those dreams into goals. That's where you finally get into the "how." For example, in order to be a #1 *New York Times* best selling author, I need to get a really amazing book published by a large publisher.

My list of goals has revenue and profit numbers, Denise retiring from her job, courses I will take this year, learning to sail, my health goals, things I want to accomplish in my business, and living at Stallworth for the entire summer.

A "bucket list" is a list of things you want to do before you die or "kick the bucket." In the movie *The Bucket List*, Morgan Freeman and Jack Nicholson were both dying of cancer and shared a hospital room. They decided to create a bucket list and pursue each one of those goals immediately. The resulting adventures were pretty outrageous.

I was traveling with Santiago recently, and he asked me, "What is one thing you want to do before you die?"

"Live at my Stallworth house," I replied.

Then he asked another question... "What if you had only one

day to live?" obviously expecting me to answer differently.

"Live at my Stallworth house for one day." I feel like I've made a difference in a lot of lives, so if I died today, I would die a happy man. Of course, Denise and Einstein (my grand puppy) would be with me that day and we would walk on the beach holding hands. I would take a long swim and think about my life. And, of course, before it was all over, I would want to see certain people that I love one last time. Then I would make a final post on social media to tell people how much I loved them and to encourage them to live their life in such a way that they could die happy like me.

Live your life like that. Live your life in such a way that if you died today, you're good with God and you're good with everyone around you. Live in such a way that you've been significant in others' lives, so you won't feel like you have to do a bunch of things to get ready to die. I'm ready. If I live another day, I get another day to have an impact in others' lives and I get to experience growing, learning, and reaching more goals and dreams.

Living in a human body can bring many physical and emotional pains. As Jesus said, "In this life you'll have trouble, but be of good cheer, I've overcome the world." Life is a journey of living, loving, and learning so you can become the person God created you to be. Life is an experience of allowing God to mold you and to show you His purpose for your life. The bonus is that we get to do some cool things while we are here.

4. CREATE A VISION BOARD. One of the most powerful ways to dream is to create a vision board. A vision board is simply a picture of your preferred future. Pictures tend to inspire more than a list. For example, one of my dreams for many years was to have a place in Destin, FL. Long before the Stallworth story, I had a poster of the Seaside, FL post office (the location where *The Truman Show* was filmed).

It was hanging in the restroom at my office, and I saw it every day. I imagined riding my bike around Seaside with a little basket on the handlebars. During the most difficult times of building my first business, that poster kept me inspired. I kept going because I knew if I could make that business profitable, I could have my dream.

It didn't matter to me the size of the place, I just wanted something in Destin of my own, so I could enjoy the crystal clear, emerald green water and white sandy beaches in the summer. It didn't matter to me how fancy it was. I get inspired when I spend time on the beach there. Eventually, I did get that place. I bought a small condo that needed a lot of updating. It felt amazing to accomplish that goal at that time.

Today, that little condo seems like such a small goal when I compare it to everything that has happened since then. But the point is that I had a VISION of riding my bike around Seaside and spending time on that beach. The picture of the cute little post office was the inspiring picture I needed to empower me to do what I needed to do to make it happen. And, by the way, the little condo ended up being a mile and a half from Seaside. When I stayed there, I rode my bike around Seaside with the little basket on the handlebars. There's an old saying that says, "Be careful what you pray for. You just might get it."

One year at our annual Destin Dream Retreat, we brought in stacks of flip-chart paper, piles of *Success* Magazines I had collected over the years, scissors, glue sticks, and multi-colored Sharpie markers. We held an evening session where everyone in the room created their own vision board. It was very powerful.

Each year, I create a vision board on the inside flap of my Ziglar Performance Planner. For 2017, I have a drawing of our Stallworth home, photos of the beach, sailboats, my family, and a photograph of myself when I was in the very best physical shape of my life. The board shows how much income I want to make this year, the things I want to learn (like how to sail), and a list of major projects I want to accomplish.

5. THE PERFECT DAY EXERCISE. The perfect day exercise can give you a powerful vision as well. Much like the day I just shared, you would answer the following questions about the most perfect day you could imagine.

Where do you wake up? Who are you with? What do you do when you first wake up? What do you do next? At lunch? In the afternoon? In the evening?

Assuming that it wasn't my last day, I would wake up at Stallworth. Have coffee. Read the Bible and pray. Take Einstein out for a walk on the beach and watch the sunrise. Come back in and do some writing and planning. Visit with Denise when she wakes up. Go out to the beach for some sun and a swim. Have lunch with Denise. After lunch it's back to the beach to read, write, and think, or I go serve at my Phenomenal You+H program (my dream for youth). In the evenings, we have dinner with friends, or host a small group.

There will also be days where I am speaking or we are serving somewhere. Denise travels with me. I do a keynote in the morning, sign books, and visit with phenomenal people who are making a difference, or that want to learn how to do so. We fly back to Stallworth. It would be a bonus if all of that happened in one day, so I never have to spend a day in a hotel for the rest of my life!

And, of course, I leave this open for the moving of the Holy Spirit. If God tells me to do something different, I want to follow His lead.

6. THE WHEEL OF LIFE. Draw the Wheel of Life with your name or initials in the middle. Write in what you want to be, do, or have in each area. You won't set specific goals yet. Just let your imagination run. See example below.

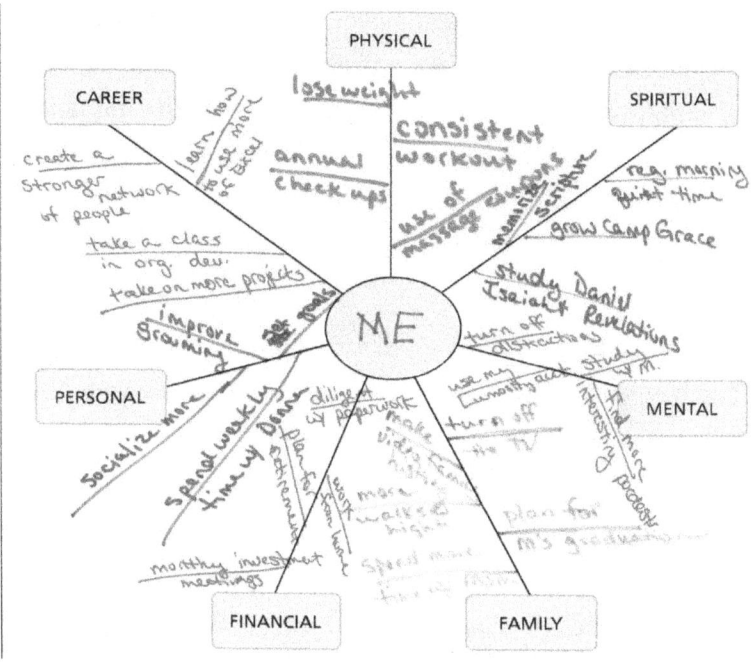

7. THE 20-YEAR VISUALIZATION EXPERIENCE. Get in a relaxed state. Put away all technology, your book, your paper, everything. Close your eyes and take a few deep breaths. Now, imagine you're at the most beautiful place you've ever seen. You're in paradise. The sky is a rich blue—not a cloud in the sky. The weather is perfect. Warm, but not too hot. There's a gentle breeze that blows across your warm skin. Take a few more deep breaths as you soak in the beauty.

You begin to notice that behind you, there's a path. Begin to walk toward the path. As you begin to walk the path, you can hear the leaves of the trees rustling in the gentle breeze. The temperature is still perfect.

As you're walking along, you begin to see a hill up ahead. You see that the path goes up the hill. It's not steep. You begin your way up the hill. As you're making your way up, you notice there is someone at the very top. You can't make out who it is yet, but as you begin to approach the top, you begin to recognize this person. This person looks very familiar to you. This person appears to be about twenty years older than you, and as you get even closer, you suddenly realize, it *is* you! It is you twenty years from now.

Talk with this older, wiser version of yourself. Have a conversation about where you've been over the last twenty years. What happened? What were some of the decisions you made? What advice does your future self have for you? Have that conversation now. Take deep breaths and take in this moment.

When you're ready, you can wind down the conversation. Don't worry, you can come back anytime. Bid your future self good-bye, and begin to make your way back down the hill. Continue on the path back to your beautiful place. Have a seat and think about the conversation you just had.

What did your future self say to you?

Take a few deep breaths and when you're ready, open your eyes.

Once you open your eyes, write down everything you remember about the conversation.

Was it emotional for you?

The first time I did it, it was very emotional. I was thin, strong, and very tan. My future self reached down and took me by the arm to help me up the hill and simply said with many tears, "We helped a lot of people." More than a conversation, it was just a time of rejoicing over the work that had been done to help others.

CHAPTER 7

DREAMS DO COME TRUE

RUDY RUETTIGER, THE REAL GUY from the movie *Rudy*, had a dream to play football for Notre Dame. The problem was that he wasn't big enough, strong enough, or smart enough to get into Notre Dame, much less play football. But his dream did come true. There are two reasons his dream came true—one, he never allowed the thought to leave his mind. Second, he worked very hard toward his dream.

Then Rudy had another dream. To make a movie about his experience. Making a movie is no easy feat. When I interviewed Rudy at Zig Ziglar's studio, he told me that he dreamt about making the movie every day. All day. And that is the key. You must put the picture in your mind and never allow it to leave.

Remember that the reaching of the dream comes as a result of seeing it in your mind first, and nourishing that vision every day. Think it. Ink it. Write it. Draw it. Talk about it. Find people to help you. If it's a worthy dream, don't abandon it. If it's something you want simply for your ego, let it go.

Not only did Rudy not abandon the dream, he worked toward that dream every day. He endured many disappointments and faced many discouragements. He worked hard for his dream.

Now that he has done the hard work, he has a lucrative career as a public speaker. I would like to note that Rudy's dream of making a movie was both personal and impersonal. The film *Rudy* is not only one of the most inspirational movies ever made, but it is one of the most watched sports movies in history.

When I was about 12 years old, I was flipping through a magazine and came across a picture of people roller-skating down the bike path at Venice Beach, CA. As I gazed at the picture, I began to daydream about what it would be like to go to California.

Of course, that sounds strange today as I might fly to California for a meeting. In fact, I flew to California just to introduce Michael Gerber for his 80th birthday party. You have no idea what is in your future. Gary Keller, co-founder of Keller-Williams, the largest residential real estate company in the country, says, "You're less than five years away from your biggest dreams and goals."

Think about where you were five years ago. Have you come a long way? If so, how did that happen? I bet you had to work hard to accomplish what you accomplished. If you're stuck, you can look back and see some things you should have done.

If you're worse off than five years ago, perhaps there was an event in your life that caused it. Maybe you did something to cause that event. Maybe it was unavoidable. Someone once mused, "There's a reason the windshield is bigger than the rearview mirror."

It doesn't matter where you've been, or where you are now, you're less than five years away from your biggest dreams and goals, as Gary said. It doesn't matter what kind of difficulties you've had. In fact, isn't it true that we grow more through difficulties and trials than we do successes? It's true.

The question is whether you will create a meaningful dream,

whether you'll nourish it, and whether you'll do the hard work to get there. Rudy worked hard to reach his dream. Zig worked hard to reach his dream. Motivational speaker Darren Hardy maintains that success is found through true grit.

Follow this success formula to reach your dream:

1. Have a compelling picture of the future. (That comes through prayer, dreaming, and thinking.)
2. Believe that you can achieve it. (Stories of others who have been successful will help you.)
3. Surround yourself with people that have already done what you want to do. (This is the greatest life lesson I could ever share with you.)
4. Take massive action every day. (More on this in an upcoming chapter.)
5. Track your results.

CHAPTER 8

Trust God. Love Others.

Jesus was once tested with this question: *"Teacher, which is the great commandment in the Law?" And He said to him, "'You shall love the Lord your God with all your heart, and with all your soul, and with all your mind.' This is the great and foremost commandment. The second is like it, 'You shall love your neighbor as yourself.' On these two commandments depend the whole Law and the Prophets." —Matthew 22:36-40*

If we just get practical about our faith and realize that we can trust the One who made us, because He IS Love, and He loves us, we can have the peace in our hearts that He will take care of us. He will give us a meaningful life.

Trust God. Pray to Him without ceasing. He knows your sins and your sorrows. He knows your dreams and desires. He made you, and He walks with you. You only have to allow Him to live through you. We are all flawed in the flesh, but we have freedom through faith.

More on that later.

The first step to get meaning out of life is to draw near to Him. When you do that, you'll have peace in your heart. The second step is to love others. Remember that all of life is about relationships. First, your relationship with God. Second, your relationship with others.

That's all you'll have when you leave this earth. All you'll take with you is your legacy. How you lived your life. Rhonda Formby wrote a song around the poem "The Dash" and sang it at my conference. The dash is the line in between the two dates on a tombstone.

I love the chorus so much that I printed it and put it on my vision board in my planner:

Who did you love?
Did you have dreams you never tried?
Who did you touch?
Those are the things you leave behind
What does it mean to you?
Your legacy, how they remember you
Oh, it's your life in one small line

Tom Ziglar challenges us to think about our legacy. What will your great-grandchildren say about you? What mark are you leaving on hearts each day? Eleanor Roosevelt penned these beautiful words:

Many people will walk in and out of your life, but only true friends will leave footprints on your heart.

Take a moment to reflect on what you believe about God. Do you trust Him? Do you trust Him with your whole life? If He created you, don't you think that He will take care of you?

Doesn't it make sense that if He made you, and He loves you, that He will take care of you? Did you know that Jesus said, "Not even a sparrow falls to the ground without God knowing about it?" Did you know that Scripture states that He knows the number of hairs on your head?

If He created billions of stars, and He loves YOU, what does that say about you? What does that say about your future?

If God put a dream in your heart, don't you think He will help you reach it? If He put the dream in your heart, don't you think He will help you? Have you read that He will never leave you nor forsake you? Do you remind yourself of that? I know I sound like I'm preaching right now, but I'm really trying to put this in practical terms. If God truly loves you that much (and He does), you can trust Him.

What about your personal dreams? Does He care about those? Does He care about your "house on the beach" (figuratively speaking)? In the Stallworth story, I shared how I had doubts that God was okay with me spending a bunch of money on a personal dream. I struggled with that. Honestly, I still struggle with having lots of stuff. I am very blessed.

John Maxwell told me one time, "When you have five houses and twelve cars, it's time to move from success to significance." He didn't mean you had to have that many houses or cars before helping others, of course. He just meant that at some point in time, the dream has to go from personal to impersonal.

In fact, it should start with the impersonal. As I was struggling with the thought of investing so much in a house, I happened to be hosting a webinar with a very successful public speaker by the name of Jim Cathcart. During the webinar warm-up before the broadcast started, I shared my feelings with him.

He began to point out how many jobs would be created as a result of building that house. And it's true. At this moment in time, the house is almost finished. Cabinets are going in next week. The real estate people had work, the county people had work, the survey people had work, the builder had work, the concrete people had work, and all the construction trades had work. Once we move in, maintenance people will have work.

Thanks to Jim, I no longer think "should I have two dream homes? Should I go on an extravagant vacation?" Instead, I think "The more money I spend, the better the economy will be, and the more those precious families who are supported by the people who build things, serve meals, or run a sailing adventure will have!"

Of course, I still give a lot to charity, too. I give to my church regularly. I donate regularly, and I have mentees in my life that I believe in, so I help them financially so they can get ahead faster.

Does God care about those people? Yes! And only He can tell you how much to give. It's all His anyway, so ask Him.

This principle is "Trust God. Love Others." This is a mantra that has served me well. When I go through difficulties, I tell myself to trust God because I know He cares for me.

And I tell myself to love others because I know it pleases God and it's the right thing to do. I also know there is a Spiritual Law that states "Give and it will be given back to you, pressed down, shaken together, and running over." Jesus told us that. It's just like planting seed.

Loving others means to give to them, be committed to them, be merciful to them, forgive them, care for them, have empathy for them, serve them, listen to them, and many other things.

Trust God and love others. When you do that, I'm convinced you'll reach more of your dreams.

CHAPTER 9

VISION WITHOUT ACTION IS A DAYDREAM

I LOVE TO DREAM. I hope you do, too. But the fact is that you can have the most exciting, most thrilling, most fantastic dream ever conceived, but if you don't take action, it will be nothing more than a daydream.

Have you ever met someone that has lots of dreams and does lots of talking, but they never do anything? You don't want to be that person. You also don't want to be the person in the second part of the proverb:

Action without vision is a nightmare.

Most people just get up every day and react to the circumstances of the day. They just exist in the media-driven, water-cooler conversation of the day. Whatever's happening in the news. Whatever circumstances come their way. They can't wait to get "off work." TGIF is the motto at the end of the week. What a miserable way to live!

And today's workplace is filled with stress from difficult relationships, and a generally selfish, and sometimes backstabbing environment. On top of it, the media instills fear rather than hope. Seventy percent of American workers are disengaged. Eighteen percent despise their jobs (their source of income), and calendars seem to be overwhelmed with too many obligations.

How do we escape that nightmare? By getting a vision. Live your life according to the vision you have. Don't live by circumstance. Like Rudy, have a vision and take action.

Your phenomenal dream will become a reality by staying focused on the vision and continually taking action. I teach small business owners that the #1 reason they don't grow or do as well as they could is because of what I call F.T.I. (Failure To Implement).

And it's the same for any individual. Would you be more successful if you could simply get more done? Sure you would. Would massive implementation take you closer to your dream? Of course it would.

So you want to replace F.T.I. with F.I.T. (Focus, Implement, and Track). Get a vision, then implement. Then track to see what worked and what didn't.

Your dream becomes a reality by taking small steps along the way. Think of your dream as an exciting destination like Hawaii. When your plane takes off for Hawaii, you know that you have a certain number of hours before you touch down in paradise. You can measure the hours. In fact, sometimes they even have a flight tracker on display.

Break your dream down into manageable goals. In order to reach my dream of living at Stallworth on my "dream beach," I had to get myself in the right position financially. To be financially "F.I.T.," I had to set some goals (focus), I had to work hard (implementation), and I had to measure my results (track). Focus. Implement. Track.

If your dream is to run a major marathon and you've never

done it before, you'll have to set some small goals first. You'll want to figure out the best place to start, like run three miles, and then you focus, implement, and track. Focus on everything you need to do to make three miles. Run the three miles, then track your time. Then you focus, implement, and track over and over again as you increase the miles.

Eventually, by staying focused and taking action toward your goal, your dream will become a reality. Phenomenal success is possible with vision plus action.

The four keys to overcome F.T.I. are…

1. Inspiration – Would you agree that you would get more done if you had more energy? If you had more passion? In their incredible book *The Power of Full Engagement*, Jim Loehr and Tony Schwartz reveal that managing energy, not time, is the key to high performance and personal renewal.

Inspiration is not the same thing as motivation. Motivation comes from external forces. Motivation is when you have a bill coming up that you don't have money for, and you have to hustle a little harder than normal. Or, the day before vacation, you're motivated to check more things off the list, so you take major action that day.

Inspiration is something that happens on the *inside*. It's the desire that is created when you finally *see* the vision. When you finally get it. Inspiration happens when you can finally *see* yourself in the picture of your preferred future.

Inspiration happens when you meet someone who started out where you are and achieved big things. For example, I went to Microsoft with John Maxwell's highest level group and met then COO, Kevin Turner. Kevin Turner is one of the few people on the planet that worked directly for Sam Walton (founder of Wal-Mart and Sam's Club) and Bill Gates (founder of Microsoft). Kevin Turner started as a *cashier* at Wal-Mart!

Walt Disney had a vision. And he took major action. Ray Kroc, founder of McDonald's franchising operation, had a vision. And he took major action. Every person mentioned here had major roadblocks and detours, but they stayed the course because they had a vision—a dream—that inspired them.

Stay around people and books, like this one, to inspire you. Inspiration is the fuel you need to move forward. In his book *Better than Good*, Zig wrote "Inspiration is the fuel of passion."

He encouraged us to:

» *Invest in Inspiration* – You and I have three kinds of resources given to us by God that we can invest in whatever we choose: time, talent, and treasure.

» *Inquire for Inspiration* – Find a mentor. Be a mentor.

» *Get Involved to Find Inspiration* – The bigger the movement is in which we choose to get involved, the more inspired we are.

» *Imagine for Inspiration* – Zig pictured himself speaking before crowds of thousands of people, knocking them dead with his humor and wisdom, and humbly receiving their standing ovations. Zig said, "I never allowed that picture to be erased from my mind. And everything I had imagined, and then some, became reality."

2. Organization – Would you agree that the more organized you are, the more likely you are to implement? It has been said that more time is wasted looking for things than any other time waster. Get your dreams and goals organized with the Ziglar Performance Planner. Draw your dream in the front inside cover and glue some inspirational photos to create your vision board there. Then fill in your dream list.

The Ziglar Performance Planner will help you keep your thoughts organized and track your success. Remember, to avoid F.T.I., you have to Focus, Implement, and Track (F.I.T.).

3. Training – Would you agree that you would get more done if you had more training in the areas you need to perform in? Of course you would. Training breeds confidence in what you are doing. It also helps you to do it more smoothly and more effectively.

For example, you don't fly an airplane with some inspiration and a manual. At least, you shouldn't! With proper training and experience, you become a safer pilot. You can go farther with training.

4. Support – Finally, would you agree that you could get more of the good things done if you had a support system around you? I've found that the most complete way to ensure implementation is to have a group of people around you to support you, to encourage you, and to hold you accountable.

As I mentioned before, we all need community. You need a phenomenal dream team to help you accomplish your phenomenal dream. If you have a dream, but no team, you have to give up the dream or build up the team.

Who are the mentors, coaches, cheerleaders, best friends, team members, faith members, or family members that will provide the support, encouragement, and accountability to help you live your dream life?

And who will you support? Who will you encourage? Who will you hold accountable? Who is on your phenomenal dream team? You can have the biggest dream in the world, but if you don't have the support to reach it, it is nothing more than a fantastic daydream.

CHAPTER 10

GO CONFIDENTLY IN THE DIRECTION OF YOUR DREAMS

THIS WELL-KNOWN QUOTE comes from philosopher Henry David Thoreau...

"Go confidently in the direction of your dreams.
Live the life you have imagined."

"If one advances confidently in the direction of his dreams, and endeavors to live the life which he has imagined, he will meet with a success unexpected in common hours."

My good friend and author, coach Michelle Prince, sometimes serves as emcee at my conferences. She was on the stage once talking about goals and dreams. Speaking of my dreams and goals coming true, she proclaimed, "I'm sure Howard could see all of this in his mind before it happened."

I saw *some* of it. I saw enough of it to get me excited and inspired. But I had no idea it would turn into everything it has. The point is that when you *go confidently* in the direction of your dreams, you'll be *met with a success unexpected* in "common" hours.

Common hours. The days when people believe they can only be great if they make it big as an entertainer or win the lottery. Very sad. You can be great right now. You can be significant right now. You can start making a difference in others' lives right now. You don't have to be great to start, but you do have to start to be great.

Over the years, I've been laughed at a lot. When I started my first company, I was part of a small industry group that met every week to talk about how to improve the industry. Some of the guys in that group had a serious case of "stinkin' thinkin'" which leads to "hardening of the attitudes" and needed a "check-up-from-the-neck-up," as Zig used to say."

Some of them hadn't shaved (it was Monday morning), and they were wearing cut-off blue jeans and flip-flops. Appropriate attire, if you're going to the beach. I arrived carrying a briefcase, wearing a sport coat, a tie, and a positive attitude. They literally laughed at me and mocked, "Who do you think you are, Zig Ziglar or somebody?"

Well, I didn't even know Zig Ziglar at the time. Most of those guys are out of business now, and the ones that still exist have a pretty miserable existence. Over the years, I became a top consultant in that industry. People still ridicule me today, but for a different reason—because I'm successful. And while having their crude little Facebook jests, they feverishly copy my material. I came across this quote recently that made me giggle: "First they laugh at you, then they copy you."

The fact is that I just did what most of them are unwilling to do. They aren't willing to do what is required to be successful. They are more comfortable getting likes and comments from their uncouth social media buddies. One of Dave Ramsey's favorite quotes is "If you're willing to live like no one else will for just a little while, you can live the rest of your life like no one else can."

I don't want to be unkind, or ungrateful, or belittle anyone in any way, but the fact is that I wear flip-flops and shorts most of the time now. Not because I'm unsuccessful and unwilling to do what's required, but because I did it.

Another dream that came true for me was to be featured in the documentary film *Zig: You Were Born To Win*. I also helped fund the film by donating money to the project. Because I'm listed as one of the "executive producers," I was able to sit in on some of the filming.

When we shot Dave Ramsey's segment, he chuckled at the notion that people have about him being an *overnight success*. "Yeah, after twenty-five years of working your tail off!"

In my fifth published book, *Phenomenal Success Stories – The Simple Path from Survival to Success to Significance*, I shared that success is simple. It's just not easy. I outlined a simple set of steps that anyone can take to be successful and significant.

I'm convinced that the only reason people aren't more successful and significant is either because they don't want to be or don't believe they can be. In either case, the root of that kind of thinking is fear.

When you have fear, you don't have confidence. Fear paralyzes your mind. To go confidently means you have to have faith. An old Indian story tells it this way…

A wise old chief told the brave, "There are two hungry wolves that live inside of you, and they are trying to devour one another. One wolf is named Fear and the other is named Faith."

"Which one wins?" asked the little brave.

"The one you feed," said the chief. You cannot reach your biggest dreams in life and live in fear. You must have faith.

Go. Confidently. *Live* the life you've imagined.

You may not see your whole dream yet. Most people don't. Your dream will change. You may only be able to see the first few feet of the path. That's okay. Go as far as you can see, and then you'll be able to see farther.

And as the rest of the quote goes, *"If one advances confidently in the direction of his dreams, and endeavors to live the life which he has imagined, he will meet with a success unexpected in common hours."*

I wrote in my journal last week on the dream beach:

"I can't believe that my dream home is almost complete. But it's almost complete because I believed."

Let me say once again that the house itself is not the point. It's not the destination. It's the journey. It's who you become. It's what you discover along the way. It's who you meet and who you help. It's the thrill of discovering uncommon success in so-called "common" hours.

CHAPTER 11

THINK AND BE PHENOMENAL

I WROTE A BOOK with this same name, so I won't re-write the book here. Since I've covered the importance of thinking and dreaming, and now we are talking about implementing—and, more important, becoming—I want to bring your attention to the subtitle of my book *Think and Be Phenomenal* which is *The 5 Levels of BEing Phenomenal.*

Level 1: Self-Awareness

You become aware of your thoughts, feelings and habits. You become aware of a new idea or a new skill you want to develop. You become aware that a change is needed.

Level 2: Willing to Change

People only change through desperation or inspiration. Depending on what you're trying to change, there's a great deal of fear behind it. The fear of losing what we have is too great to move past this level.

Level 3: Controlled Attention

After getting through the FEAR of Level 2, you move into the stage of Controlled Attention. You apply a great deal of focus and attention to the new skill, idea, or habit. It's uncomfortable because you've never done it before, and your body and emotions are screaming at you like a baby crying for a bottle because they've become so accustomed to the old you.

Level 4: Commitment

When you become committed to a new lifestyle, habit, or routine, you become more persistent and consistent. You are now hitting stride and getting results. Your confidence increases because of that.

Commitment is not the end. It's just the level you must get to in order to enter Level 5...

Level 5: Character

Level 5 is when you have truly become the person you want to be. Level 5 is when your habits and values have changed. Your life and destiny are determined by your values. You do what you value and you value what you do. Therefore, your habits control you. The character level is where you've successfully shed the old habit and replaced it with a new one.

How do you know you've reached this level? Only time will tell. You might think you're in the Character Level, but you've just been in the Commitment Level for a long time.

You Keep Each Level as You Move Up

Something interesting to note is that each of the levels stays with you as you move up. For example, self-awareness runs through all of the levels. Self-awareness is the key factor to all of the levels. At Willing to Change, you will stay aware of your thoughts, feelings and actions as you uncover the fears, the roadblocks, and the challenges *that you are going through as you decide whether doing the hard work of Level 2 is worth it or not.*

When you move to Level 3, your Self-Awareness and Willingness to Change must stay intact in order to stay Focused. In order to operate in Level 4, you must remain Aware, Willing to Change and Focused. Level 5 happens automatically when you stay in Commitment long enough.

The Most Phenomenal News of All

The best news is that you can change. It's difficult today because many of us didn't learn the basic disciplines as children, as children once did. Modern conveniences allowed the media to think for us and caused us to be lazy thinkers, full of fear and doubt. Don't let that happen to you.

Remember who you are (and Whose you are). You are a phenomenal product created to do phenomenal things and to have a phenomenal life. You were born to win. You were designed for accomplishment, engineered for success, and endowed with the seeds of greatness.

You can do this!

We all go through these five levels when reaching for a dream. As you begin to move toward your dream, you'll find out a lot about yourself. You'll realize that you are going through the five levels of becoming the person you really want to be.

Becoming the person you were created to be is the ultimate dream, and when you become that person, you'll consistently do the things you need to do to turn your new dream into your new reality.

CHAPTER 12

BE TRANSFORMED BY THE RENEWING OF YOUR MIND

As I mentioned earlier in this book, man is designed with a spirit, a soul (mind, will, and emotion), and body. As you fight your flesh (cravings of the body) with your faith (God's Spirit inside your spirit), your mind, will, and emotion are in the cross fire of the two. Your mind reminds you that you should do a particular thing, or it tells you that you shouldn't do a particular thing, but your flesh wages war through your emotions. The flesh pulls on the emotions, and God speaks to your mind.

As the Apostle Paul lamented, "I find that there's a war inside—I don't do the things I wish and I do the things I don't wish to do. Wretched man am I! Who can rescue me from this body of death!"

The Truth will set you free. You will be renewed, shaped, and ultimately transformed by renewing your mind—by washing it in the Truth. The problem is that we all get stinkin' thinkin' and we need a check-up-from-the-neck-up, as Zig used to say.

We need people around us to remind us of who we are, Whose we are, where we are going, and to hold us accountable to be the person we say we want to be. This is a daily battle. This is why we need community. We need a group of people around us that have the same vision and values as we have.

Surround yourself with people who will support you, encourage you, and hold you accountable. Surround yourself with people who support your dream. Surround yourself with people who will continuously remind you of the Truth.

Every day, we must be reminded of the Truth.

The Truth will set you free.

Doubt and fear kill more dreams than failure ever will. When you feel fear or doubt welling up inside of you, remind yourself of the Truth. If you are a believer in Christ, you have been set free. You have the mind of Christ. Jesus told us "the Truth will set you free." He also said He is "The Way, The Truth, and The Life." We have the mind of Christ.

God's Spirit is inside you if you're a believer in Him. He speaks the Truth in your spirit. But you have an enemy, too. Satan, the devil, the one who roams the earth seeking to steal, kill, and destroy, wants your mind.

The battle is for your mind. Whoever controls the mind wins. Satan tempts us through the flesh and through our emotions. He is a liar. He uses every tool he can to lie to you. He uses other people, the media, your own imaginations and fears and demons to tell you lies.

The Scripture says our struggle is not against flesh and blood, but against the powers and principalities that dwell in high places. If you know Christ, you have a secret weapon: The Holy Spirit inside of you. He is your comforter, your helper in time of need.

One of the things the enemy loves to do is use your sins against you. The thoughts you've had about others and the things you've done in the past. Everyone sins, but if you know Jesus, God has removed your sin as far as the east is from the west. In case you don't get that, the east never meets the west. If you head either direction, you'll never meet the other one. The same is not true for north and south.

In other words, He does not remember your sins. But Satan does. He is the accuser of the brethren. Jesus is your Advocate.

CHAPTER 13

Pray Without Ceasing. Be Anxious for Nothing

Remember that God is always there. Always be lifting your thoughts up to God. You can talk to Him any day, any time. He loves you. He cares for you. And He is interested in every detail of your life. He knows how many hairs you have on your head. He created you. He made you to have fellowship with Him. You are His child. He wants to talk to you.

I love the book of Philippians, and one of my favorite passages is Chapter 4:5b-9...

The Lord is near. Be anxious for nothing, but in everything by prayer and supplication with thanksgiving let your requests be made known to God. And the peace of God, which surpasses all comprehension, will guard your hearts and your minds in Christ Jesus.

Finally, brethren, whatever is true, whatever is honorable, whatever is right, whatever is pure, whatever is lovely, whatever is of good repute, if there is any excellence and if anything worthy of praise, dwell on these things. The things you have learned and received and heard and seen in me, practice these things, and the God of peace will be with you.

And Hebrews 4:16...

> *Therefore let us draw near with confidence to the throne of grace, so that we may receive mercy and find grace to help in time of need.*

Remember, you can have confidence because God loves you. You don't have anything to fear because God is Love. If you know Him, you are in the palm of His hand. As the song goes, "He walks with you, He talks with you, and He calls you His own."

You can lift your burdens up to Him anytime. When you get in your dreaming place, just talk to Him and listen. When I walk my beach, I talk to God a lot. Remember that it's thinking, dreaming, and praying. Since no one is around, I can talk to God out loud.

Whether it's an audible prayer or a silent prayer, He hears you, He loves you, and He wants the best for you, just like any loving father would, only better. He cares for you!

Speaking of praying, the way you start your day is important. Make it a habit to begin your conversation with God as soon as you wake up. Be aware of your thoughts and lift them up to God constantly throughout the day.

Here's how I pray:

1. I thank Him for Who He is. I thank Him for everything He has done for me and what He is doing in my life. I thank Him for all the people He has put in my life. Denise, Christian, my team, my clients, and my friends.
2. I ask for forgiveness for my sins. One thing to keep in mind is that as a believer, your sin has been forgiven forever. As far as the east is from the west, as we covered earlier. However, when you sin, confess it to God so that it doesn't hinder you. The fact that you live in a human body means you are prone to sin. Everyone sins. Scripture teaches that God forgives you and cleanses your soul when you confess your sin to Him.

3. I ask Him for wisdom and anointing. I ask Him to give me a vision for my life. I ask Him to help me. I ask Him to lead me and to guide me. I ask Him to help me help people.
4. I lift up others to Him. I have a specific list of people that He has put in my heart that I pray for every day. I have been praying for some of them for years. Most of them don't even know I pray for them.
5. I ask Him to take care of my needs. I pray for my companies to be profitable, and I pray for the personal dreams and impersonal dreams that I have.

This prayer continues throughout the day. I'm constantly praying throughout the day. One time I was at a conference, and I was walking to my rental car in the parking lot, praying out loud. I didn't realize a colleague was sitting in his car eating a sandwich with his window down. I told him "Well, now you know it's for real." He smiled.

I also read a chapter out of the Bible every morning. It only takes five minutes or so. If you start your day reading the Word of God and with prayer, it changes everything because you're setting your mind on the right things first. However you start your day tends to influence the rest of the day. Getting your mind and heart right, and beginning that conversation with God, is very important. Keep it going throughout the day, every day.

Here's a model of prayer that Jesus left for us. Notice that He warned us not to use meaningless repetition, but what did we humans do? We turned the Lord's Prayer into a chant! Talk to Him as a little child. Notice that He also knows what you need before you ask Him. If that's true, why do we pray? Because He wants to talk with us! He wants to hear from us, just like a loving father wants to hear from his child.

Here's Matthew 6:7-13. Use this model to guide your prayer...

[7] *"And when you are praying, do not use meaningless repetition as the Gentiles do, for they suppose that they will be heard for their many words.* [8] *So do not be like them; for your Father knows what you need before you ask Him.*

[9] *"Pray, then, in this way:*
'Our Father who is in heaven, (puts things into perspective)
'Hallowed be Your name.
[10] *'Your kingdom come.*
'Your will be done,
'On earth as it is in heaven.
[11] *'Give us this day our daily bread.*
[12] *'And forgive us our debts, as we also have forgiven our debtors.*
[13] *'And do not lead us into temptation, but deliver us from evil. For Yours is the kingdom and the power and the glory forever. Amen.'"*

Two Chairs

Ziglar friend and associate Bob Beaudine wrote a book called *2 Chairs: The Secret that Changes Everything*.

He writes:

"In this world you will have trouble. Count on it!

"It might be something small or something big, but you know you don't have an answer. You've come to a realization there is a limit to what you can do alone. For such times as these, **2 Chairs** asks three vital questions:

Chapter 13

"Does God know your situation?"

"Is it too hard for Him to handle?

"Does He have a good plan for you?"

Bob then recommends "meeting" with God every morning in two chairs. One for you and one for God. Sit down and talk to Him. He is your Father who loves you dearly. He knows what's going on in your life. He knows what's coming. He knows everything.

CHAPTER 14

I Can Do All Things Through Him Who Strengthens Me

As you get closer to the end of this book, you see that I have been influenced greatly by my Christian faith, and I love the Word of God. Especially the book of Philippians.

This Scripture, Philippians 4:13, is often quoted, but the context is usually lost. In this verse, Paul was actually talking about money. He states that he knows what it's like to have money and not to have money.

As Bob Beaudine points out in his book, "You will have trouble in this life. Either you're just coming out of trouble, you're in trouble right now, or you're heading into trouble." When Bob proclaimed that from the stage at my conference, it had been a long time since I had trouble. I felt secure. I thought to myself, "I sure hope he isn't right!" Sure enough, just in less than a year, trouble came!

Of course, Bob got that from Jesus, because Jesus told us "In this world you will have trouble. But be of good cheer as I have overcome the world."

Chapter 14

Zig used to say, "I've had problems when I had money and I've had problems without money, and I've learned that if you're going to have problems, it's better to have money when you have them!" Money can't solve all the problems in life, but it can fund your dream if you think about it the right way.

Growing up on welfare, I know what it's like not to have money. Fortunately, today I have money. And because of that, I've been able to reach many personal and impersonal dreams. I've been able to build dream homes, travel the world, have some pretty cool stuff, and do some pretty cool things.

But nothing compares to helping others that don't have money. I've given a lot of money away and am able to support a lot of great causes. I *love* to give away money.

Talking about money brings up all sorts of weird emotions. We are all taught things about money that are untrue. And if we aren't taught them consciously, we've received unconscious messages about being wealthy.

When was the last time you saw a movie where the wealthy person was the good guy? And if he was the hero of the movie, he probably had some pretty bad vices and wasn't the most moral person around. Why do we use the term "filthy rich" when we refer to someone with money?

Of course, this is when everyone wants to run to the Bible, whether they go to it for anything else or not. They love to quote "The love of money is the root of all evil." Loving money is the actual point, and the literal translation is all sorts of evil.

I recommend reading *Thou Shalt Prosper* by Rabbi Daniel Lapin to find out what the Scripture actually says about money. And it would be a good time to remind ourselves that the values we have picked up along the way may or may not be serving us well. Examine every thought and every philosophy you have with the truth. Remember, the truth will set you free.

From growing up on welfare, to starting my own business, to a financial life I could have only dreamed of, I have developed my own money philosophy. You would be well served to develop yours as well, because you will not reach your personal or impersonal dreams without understanding how money relates to you.

The first question is… how much money are you supposed to make? How much are you supposed to have? I love asking that question in my seminars.

I get various responses, but here's my take: You need to make the amount of money that is required to fulfill your vision. Jesus didn't own anything, but money was involved in the mission. Otherwise, there wouldn't have been a money bag to be stolen by Judas. People gave to the mission, but Jesus didn't need money because He only had an impersonal dream, and He had complete faith, seeing how He was the Son of God and all.

Someone once remarked that it cost a lot of money to keep Gandhi poor! The point is that your dream has an investment attached to it. One of the ten questions John Maxwell asks in his book *Put Your Dream to the Test* is the *Cost* question. In fact, he said it will cost more than you think.

That has certainly been my experience. In order to fund your dream, you need money. Here's my money philosophy:

1. Make a lot. Since I want to do a lot, I need to make a lot of money. I have many dreams and many goals, so I need lots of funding!

2. Give a lot. First, I give a portion of my income to my local church automatically. Second, I help various ministries and

causes as well as people who are in need, or that I want to invest in.

3. Invest a lot. I've always been pretty good at *making* money, but not very good at *keeping* it! I learned the value of being debt-free and I've realized the value of investing. Understanding how to make your money work for you is very valuable in reaching more of your dreams and goals, and being smart with your money gives you more to help others with as well. Being broke and/or in debt doesn't help anyone except for the finance companies!

4. Spend a lot! Okay, I admit it. I love to spend money. It's a thrill to buy stuff. But I don't buy stuff I can't afford any longer, and since I do items 1 through 3, I can spend a lot, too. And there is a positive reason to spend money. It helps our economy. The bottom line is that your bottom line funds the dream.

CHAPTER 15

Stay Humble

Writing a chapter on humility is awkward for me any way you slice it, but especially after talking so much about money! One of the unexpected blessings that has come with my work has been to speak to Amish communities. The Amish seem to be the epitome of humility.

Recently, just before I took the stage in front of a few hundred Amish, an elder Amish man struck up a conversation with me. "Are you our speaker today?"

"Yes sir," I answered.

"Are you a Christian?"

"Yes sir."

"Well, do you tell people that you get your information from the Bible?"

"Yes sir," I repeated, nervously, not knowing what was coming next.

"Well, I sure wish other speakers would do that!" he exclaimed. He then went on a rant about humility and how all of us have so much pride. I agreed with him, but grew even more nervous as I was about to take the stage, and this man got me feeling like there might be some kind of exorcism if I didn't give the right message.

Chapter 15

Never mind the fact that I've spoken to the Amish many times and they have always been gracious and kind, and I've never been taken to the woodshed.

The fact remained, however, that here I was in an expensive suit and tie, sporting a Florida tan amongst the Amish and their plain clothing. I began to feel self-conscious. As I was sharing from the stage, I noticed he was diligently taking notes and listening intently. And, of course, after the speech, who do you think I sought out first? My new mentor, of course!

"So, what would you have changed about my presentation?" I inquired.

"Everything!" he shouted.

"Everything!"

"What do you mean?" I shot back.

"You got about as much pride as I do!" He proclaimed as he slapped his chest.

Pride? In an *Amish* man? Yes, even the Amish have pride. We all do. It turns out that he is converted Amish. Originally from Georgia. This explained why he was a little more outspoken than those born Amish.

Turns out that the Amish are just like everyone else. They have pride, guilt, fear, and all of the other emotions as the rest of us mortals. One of my supporters in Amish country owns a Christian bookstore, and he gave me a book that outlines the history of Holmes County, Ohio, the largest Amish community in America. It reveals several splits from the norm, the first one that was triggered by the murder of an infant! I never expected to learn *that*! The message here (other than the fact that I'm truly naïve), is that when you're showered with blessings, you can become prideful and forget Who got you where you are. My message from the Amish man was to stay humble. Say no to pride.

The night before Zig Ziglar appeared on stage at my conference (another dream come true), we were having a private dinner of about fourteen people. Zig looked around the room and sensed an air of pride as we rejoiced in our successes and accomplishments and said, "Just remember, none of us got to where we are by ourselves."

He was also known to say on many occasions, "If you ever see a turtle on top of a fencepost, you can be guaranteed he didn't get there by himself!"

CHAPTER 16

LIVE IN FREEDOM EVERY DAY

I HAVE AN ACRONYM for L.I.F.E.
Living

In

Freedom

Everyday

There's no freedom in being stuck. There's no freedom in carrying around undue stress. There's no freedom in not having peace with your Creator. There's no freedom in not having phenomenal relationships in your life, being stuck in a job you hate, being broke, in debt, and not having joy in your life.

Yet, that's exactly where many people seem to live today! How is it that we live in the most "free" country in the world, where we have such abundance, and we are so unhappy?

The media deals out fear on a minute-by-minute basis; we seem to be overwhelmed, tired, and stressed-out. How can we live in freedom in this society?

Bad news sells. Therefore, the media must have sensational headlines and stories to grab your interest. Fear sells better than anything. "21 people die in a bus accident in Arizona." "Landslide kills 3." "Terror attack in Paris."

News appeals to your base nature, which is your flesh, and your flesh is designed to respond to fear to keep you safe. The problem is that you're receiving thousands of messages of fear each and every day.

Then there's the soap opera news… which entertainer is getting divorced today, or what bad thing did they do that we obviously need to know about!

And let's not leave out Dateline and 48 Hours and the murder mysteries. Where did we get so many murder stories?

What about crime shows? If it's not real, why don't we just manufacture it? Why not? That's how you get ratings, after all!

Our children today are seeing things on their screens that no adult should ever even see. Is it possible that this is contributing to the ONE HUNDRED PERCENT increase in child suicides in the last decade? The *Wall Street Journal* reported that the biggest sector was among teenage girls.

The image of a woman has been so skewed over the past few decades to the point that most young girls hate the way they look. Cyberbullying and the pressure of looking beautiful is too much for many of them to bear.

This is one reason my burden for young people has grown. Adults know better. But children believe what their emotions tell them. Children today are mostly raised by strangers in the media. And their job is to scare us to death.

Korea, Russia, China, Iraq, Afghanistan. Terror attacks, crooked politicians, corporate scandal, the plight of the poor, and more and more fear.

Every day. Every moment. The lobbies of just about every hotel and restaurant have screens. Mostly bad news. And if it's not bad news, it's entertainment or sports. And we've laced each and every one of them with crude adult humor, including so-called family shows.

Denise and I were having lunch with a friend of hers once, and as I lamented about the condition of our society, the woman scolded me and said, "Oh, Howard, don't be such a prude!" The last time I checked, prudence was a positive virtue. And that woman, although wealthy, lives an empty, hollow life.

My personal opinion is that we're being conditioned just like the proverbial frog in boiling water. We self-medicate with counseling, entertainment, drugs, alcohol, fake and/or dysfunctional relationships to try to get along in life. Is it possible that our media intake is taking more of a toll on us than we realize? I believe it is.

Am I being overly sensitive, or am I seeing something that others are being blinded by? Is it possible that the terrible news that's constantly in our face is bleeding into our subconscious minds and creating a hidden fear that keeps us from walking in faith? I think so. And I think Scripture is clear on it. This is why I avoid television and media as much as possible.

Freedom is a result of faith. Freedom is a result of continually renewing your mind. Living in Freedom Everyday comes from spending time with God. It comes from setting our minds on the things that are pure, the things that are holy, and the things that are above. Heavenly things rather than earthly things. Fill your mind with the pure, the powerful, and the positive, and you'll experience more freedom rather than fear.

When you understand that there are two places that only you and God alone can touch—your mind and your heart—no one can make you feel bad. Only you or God can do that. No one can make you bitter or unkind. Only you can do that.

When things don't go well, we tend to immediately blame someone else or to blame our circumstances. Sometimes we blame ourselves, or worse, we get mad at God.

Freedom is found in Faith. Sometimes it's difficult to trust God. It's hard to forgive others and even harder to forgive ourselves. But Faith is where freedom is found. Trust God's Truth. The Truth will set you free.

Many people Live In Fear Everyday, rather than living in Freedom. Fear is not from God, and has no place in our lives, but the fact is we all experience fear.

There is no fear in love. Love casts out all fear, according to the Scripture. And remember the first principle: God *is* Love. So, where does fear come from? It comes from our flesh. When we operate in fear, we are operating from feelings rather than facts.

Fear produces all sorts of fantasies. We imagine all sorts of calamities that never happen and that many times are not even real. God gave humans a fantastic imagination, but instead of using it to create, we use it to imagine the worst. We live in a fallen world. We showed up into a fearful, fleshly world.

Fear kills dreams. But when we operate by Faith, love God and others, and believe that we can become the person we were created to be, that we can do the things we are called to do and to have the life we want to have, we can feel the freedom. All human beings experience fear. Successful people just know how to deal with it.

Also, keep in mind that there are many hidden fears inside of you that have been collected since you were a child that you may never fully be aware of. And we have some level of fear built in for protection. If we didn't have any fear at all, every one of us would probably be dead!

THE FEAR BEHIND THE FEAR EXERCISE

Here's what I do when I experience fear…

First, I do a self-coaching exercise called the "fear behind the fear." You can do this audibly (probably best to be alone when talking out loud to yourself. I'm just sayin'), or you can journal it. When you feel fear creeping up in your mind, try to identify the fear behind the fear. Then the fear behind that fear. Then the fear behind that fear and so on. You'll see where this ends up and why the fear is so ridiculous.

Here's a simple example: I had a coaching client who was afraid of making marketing calls to potential referral partners. When I inquired what was keeping her from making the call, she revealed that she was afraid to make the stops. I decided to do the "fear behind the fear" exercise with her.

"What's the fear behind making the calls?" I inquired.

"Because they may not like me?"

"And if they don't like you?"

"They won't refer my services."

"And if they don't use your services?"

"Then I won't make any money."

"And if you don't make any money?"

"I won't be able to feed my kids!" She exclaimed.

The next line of questioning went like this: "So, let me get this straight… currently these businesses don't refer you, correct?"

"Correct," she muttered.

"So you aren't making any money from them anyway, right?" Realizing where I was heading, she reluctantly answered with a sigh, "Right."

I continued... "Can I ask you another question... In all the years, have your kids *ever* gone hungry?" Point made. Can you see how illogical fear is? And it shows up like this in all kinds of relationships.

I've come to believe that all fear is based in a poor self-image. The remedy for a poor self-image is unconditional love. No human is capable of unconditional love consistently, but God is.

Live. In. Freedom. Everyday.

Know who you are.

Know Whose you are.

Know you are loved.

Interestingly, author Kevin Hall writes in his book, *Aspire*, that the word "believe" means to be loved.

BE LOVED because you *ARE* LOVED.

CHAPTER 17

MY GOD WILL SUPPLY ALL YOUR NEEDS ACCORDING TO HIS RICHES IN GLORY IN CHRIST JESUS

THE APOSTLE PAUL instructed us to be content with food and covering. In other words, if you have food and you have covering, be satisfied with that. I'll be the first to admit that I struggle with that. Several years ago, Hurricane Ike hit the Houston area and we were without power for ten days.

Sponge baths and candles got old pretty quickly. But that experience reminded me to be grateful for seemingly simple things, like electricity and running water. When we realize that an estimated 880 million people on the planet don't have clean drinking water, we should feel blessed and grateful.

Let us remind ourselves that God provides. He always has and He always will. Whatever you need, He will give it to you. He will never leave you nor forsake you. He has you in the palm of His hand.

When I walk on my dream beach, I am reminded of His greatness. I thank Him for saving me. I thank Him for my family.

I thank Him for those He has placed in my life to support me, encourage me, and to hold me accountable. I thank Him for the phenomenal favor He has given me. I thank Him for the dreams He has given me, and those He has allowed me to have. I thank Him for the material things He has allowed me to use while I'm here on the planet.

Zig said out of all the attitudes one can acquire, surely the attitude of gratitude is by far the most important and most life-changing. Gratitude casts out fear because it's an act of love.

When I realize that God has already supplied my every need, spiritually, emotionally, mentally, physically, and materially, it gives me peace in my heart. It gives me hope. It inspires me. It makes me want to be more generous. It makes me want to help more people know God. It makes me want to help others have what I have.

When people ask me how I'm doing, I used to say "phenomenal," of course. But then I started hanging around Ziglar. When people asked Zig how he was doing, he would say "better than good," so I changed my response to "better than phenomenal." Then our Inner Circle Community shortened it to "BTP."

Then, in classic, crazy Howard style, I started adding letters. When someone asks me how I'm doing today, I might just break out with "BTP OTT WCEB LTD OTC!"

That stands for Better Than Phenomenal, Over The Top, Who Could Ever Believe, Living The Dream, Off the Chain!

The five-year-old daughter of one of our most faithful coaching clients, Alyse Makarewicz, says this when I ask her how she's doing:

"It's a once-in-a-lifetime phenomenal day!"

Chapter 17

I often wonder why God has been so good to me. I don't deserve it more than anyone else. I don't feel that I'm any better than anyone else, and certainly not more qualified, but one of the reasons I say I'm doing BTP, OTT, etc., is because of the phenomenal God stories that have taken place in my life. Some of these I've written about in the past. Others I have not.

PHENOMENAL GOD STORIES

Weird things happen to me. I get visions that come true, and seemingly off-the-wall, incredible, and sometimes hard-to-believe things happen to me.

For example, in my first book *7 Secrets of a Phenomenal L.I.F.E.*, I shared the miracle of how I came to know God. I shared how God spoke to me audibly in a prayer meeting. A miracle happened on my father's death bed. When I started Phenomenal Products, God spoke to me through a series of events that confirmed I was supposed to do this work. You can read those stories at www.howardpartridge.org.

When I first came to know my former partner and current Admin Director Scott Zack, we drove to Dallas together from Houston. On the way there, a conversation about God came up. We stopped for gas and the exact Scripture I was sharing with him had been stuck to the bathroom mirror on a mailing label. He ended up coming to know Christ and I wanted to tell him to get baptized, but I felt the Holy Spirit tell me not to. A vision came to me one Monday morning (in my mind), and I saw Scott getting baptized, but there was a woman and a girl with him.

When I arrived at the office, he says, "Guess what I did this weekend?"

"You got baptized." I responded.

"How did you know?" he asked with surprise.

"Who got baptized with you?" I questioned.

"Dawn (his wife) and Sherri (their daughter)," he reported, obviously curious how I knew.

We have a friend who owned a series of Indian restaurants. Denise and I followed him from restaurant to restaurant for many years. I tried to talk to Ashok about Christ many times, but he wasn't interested. Meanwhile, his son came to know Christ. One day I was sitting at a red light, and I sensed I was "supposed" to go to Café India. God or not, you don't have to convince me to get Ashok's Indian food. I'm *always* up for *that*. The restaurant wasn't quite open yet, but Ashok immediately came to the glass door and unlocked it to let me in.

I could tell something was wrong. He looked pale and worried. "I'm glad you're here, Howard. I need to talk to you." I couldn't imagine what was wrong. He began to tell me that Jesus Himself visited him in his bedroom at four a.m. that day. He detailed the vision, which included Jesus dressed in white with gold sashes, leading an army of angels.

Although it was dark outside, the room was brightly lit from the vision and there was a buzzing sound. The he saw a tree trunk with no bark, and Jesus inscribed "I am the only Son of the only God in the whole world" on it. As you can imagine, I was bewildered by it all.

I drew a simple diagram on a cocktail napkin (I learned this from one of my early mentors) that explains the gospel of Christ, and he insisted that I baptize him, which I did. In fact, I've baptized several people in my pool and "led" many people to Christ.

Chapter 17

On an airplane once, I was sitting next to a lady who obviously traveled a lot. I had been upgraded to first class and she was the stereotypical first-class traveler, dressed in black, with black leather carry-ons tagged with a laminated business card.

But she seemed really nervous. I was exhausted from teaching an all-day workshop, and as I settled into my seat to take a nap, I heard a silent voice tell me that I was supposed to talk to her about God. I hate to admit that I drifted off to sleep, but when I woke up, I felt the nudge again.

I began making small talk "Do you travel much?"

"Oh yes, all the time, but I get really nervous about flying."

We made some small talk, and I suppose I could have pounced on the subject of fear and peace, but I didn't feel that was it. I got nothing from her that I felt I could connect to, so I said a silent prayer, "God, you're gonna have to help me here. I don't know what to say." In my spirit I heard, "Ask her about her mother," and I sensed something about silver jewelry.

"Is your mom still alive?" I began.

"Yes, I just saw her today."

"What kind of work does she do?" I inquired, hoping it would be the jewelry business.

"She doesn't work."

UGH! Finally, I just blurted out,

"Lady, I don't know how to tell you this, but I'm a believer in Jesus Christ, and I feel like God is telling me to talk to you, and the only thing I'm getting is something about your mother and silver jewelry."

Her jaw dropped.

"My mother just came back from Taos today and brought me a bunch of silver jewelry," she exclaimed.

I was just as dumbfounded as she. I shared the message with her and sent her some stuff in the mail a few days later and never heard from her again. I'm not sure whatever happened to her card, but who knows, maybe she'll be in heaven one of these days.

A few years ago, I got a call from my sister that she, my mother, and my aunt would be in Houston with a whole day to kill. Excited to take them out on the town, I blocked out the whole day. They arrived the night before, and when everyone was up the next morning, I surveyed them to see how they wanted to use the day. Houston has great restaurants, shopping, museums, and events—just about anything one might want to do.

My mother goes, "Is there a Goodwill around here?" Of course, you have to understand that being from "Lower Alabama" it's pronounced Guuudwheeeeuul." I was curious what they needed from Goodwill that we couldn't get somewhere else. "We just wanna browse." *Browse* at Goodwill? I sometimes forget that my mama used to take us to the day-old bread store and that most things she has purchased probably came from some place like that. But today, she's with *me*. We can go *anywhere* and buy *anything* within reason. But no, off to Goodwill we go.

Bored stiff, walking around Goodwill and trying to get used to the odor in the store that I assume must come from the aging of the stock, I found myself in front of the bookcase, of course. I began thinking there must be people who are struggling that come in that store—people who need a break—people who need a book like this one. Why couldn't Goodwill have their own book? Why couldn't they have a book that encourages people? *The Goodwill Story*, I thought to myself, would be a good title (no pun intended).

Chapter 17

I shared it with the girls, and they just rolled their eyes. I think someone muttered, "Oh, Howard." Then they went back to browsing. The idea didn't leave my mind, and I actually researched and visited Goodwill to find out what the Goodwill Story was.

Little did I know the entire organization is about providing jobs to those with physical limitations. The CEO at the time was blind, as a matter of fact. One of my previous employees has a son with Tourette Syndrome. He works at Goodwill.

Although nothing came of the idea (mainly because I didn't pursue it), a crazy thing did happen. About two weeks later, I got a phone call out of the blue. "Howard, I see you're coming to town to do a seminar, and I'd like to take you out for the biggest steak in North Carolina," the person on the other end of the phone offered.

"Why? What's your story?" I tossed back.

"Well, I lost my job last year and ran out of money. I was living in a ten-by-ten bedroom in my brother-in-law's house with my wife and two kids. I went to Goodwill looking for work boots and found one of your manuals. I bought it for twenty-five cents and started a business. I've done three hundred thousand dollars in less than a year. That's why I want to treat you to a steak dinner." Seriously, what are the chances of that? So, I went to North Carolina. He and his wife took me out for a steak dinner and told me the whole story.

What do these stories mean? To me, they tell me that God is real. That vision is real, that dreams are real.

Christmas of 2015 was approaching, and Denise kept asking me what I wanted for Christmas. I told her I wanted a stand-up paddleboard. "Those are expensive," she quipped. It's not that Denise doesn't have money, it's that she is very smart with her money, and that's why she has it!

She encouraged me to find a used one or find one on sale. Wanting to please her and honor her good judgment in the area of finances, even though I hate buying anything used, I looked around half-heartedly and never found anything I liked.

I had procrastinated so long that by Christmas Eve I had resigned myself to look for one after Christmas. On Christmas Eve, I was at the Marshall's department store picking up some stocking stuffers for Denise and Christian. As I rounded the corner with my shopping cart, I noticed a paddleboard leaning against the wall with a giant "CLEARANCE" sign on it.

I asked a clerk about it, and she immediately reacted with "my manager *really* wants to get rid of that thing!"

I was overjoyed that I could get a paddleboard *and* honor Denise's faithfulness in frugalness (that has blessed me for many years). "Bring the manager over." I quickly shot back.

As the manager and I began to negotiate, he finally revealed that the cash register would allow a maximum of 41% off. The board was on clearance for $599.00, which was already in Denise's comfort range. "Do it." I authorized. When I got to the counter to check out, the cashier advised me that if I signed up for their store credit card that I would get an additional 10% off and 5% back on my first statement. I was giddy over the whole thing.

But I still needed a paddle to go with the board. Some of the paddles I had seen were between a hundred and two hundred dollars, but I preferred a simple kayak paddle that I could use when I kneel on the board. That type of paddle can be used when you stand up, even though it's a little awkward. No big deal. I'll get one of those after Christmas.

The next day, Christmas morning, I was walking along the

Chapter 17

dream beach and noticed something that had washed up onto the shore. As I got closer, I realized it was a kayak paddle! What are the chances of that? As I got closer, I noticed that it was new, as the price tag was still attached. And what store was the price tag from? Marshall's!

CHAPTER 18

SEE YOU AT THE TOP

ZIG'S FIRST MEGA-BEST-SELLING book was called *See You at the Top*. His closing statement in all of his speeches was "And I'll see you, and yes, I really do mean you… at the top." Later on, he published a book called O*ver The Top*, so, of course, he added that.

When you follow the principles in this book, I believe you'll be at the top. What does it mean to be at the top? Zig Ziglar created a list of what "At the Top" means…

You clearly understand that failure is an event, not a person, that yesterday ended last night, and today is your brand new day.

You have made friends with your past, are focused on the present, and optimistic about your future.

You know that success doesn't make you and failure doesn't break you.

You are filled with faith, hope, and love; you live without anger, greed, guilt, envy, or thoughts of revenge.

You are mature enough to delay gratification and shift your focus from your rights to your responsibilities.

You know that failure to stand for what is morally right is the prelude to being the victim of what is criminally wrong.

You are secure in who you are, so you are at peace with God and in fellowship with man.

You have made friends of your adversaries and have gained the love and respect of those who know you best.

You understand that others can give you pleasure, but genuine happiness comes when you do things for others.

You are pleasant to the grouch, courteous to the rude, and generous to the needy.

You love the unlovable, give hope to the hopeless, friendship to the friendless, and encouragement to the discouraged.

You can look back in forgiveness, forward in hope, down in compassion, and up with gratitude.

You know that "he who would be the greatest among you must become the servant of all."

You recognize, confess, develop, and use your God-given physical, mental, and spiritual abilities to the glory of God and for the benefit of mankind.

You stand in front of the Creator of the universe and He says to you, "Well done, thou good and faithful servant."

CONCLUSION

"I ALMOST QUIT"

EARL NIGHTINGALE penned these words... "Never give up on a dream because of the time it will take to accomplish it. The time will pass anyway." I wish I had known about that quote in 2009, when I almost quit Phenomenal Products.

Just thinking about that makes me sick. Especially when I think about all the people this work has helped. The fact is that I felt like quitting at some point in the journey on all of the big goals and dreams listed in this book.

But when I get those feelings, I simply remind myself that it is a calling. It's not an option. When you find your passion, and you're living your purpose, and you live with a sense of destiny, you just can't quit. It's the reason you were born.

I hope you find your purpose. I hope you find your calling. Remember that dreams are realized through plain ol' hard work. Sometimes really hard work. You may feel like quitting. You will fail. But I believe that if you follow the 17 principles in this book, along with those that God gives you, you'll be able to live a phenomenal dream life and reach your phenomenal destiny.

Please let me know how your journey is going. Reach out to me on my social channels or by e-mail. For now, let me summarize this book...

Conclusion

God is Love and He loves you unconditionally. He made you in His image. He made you to have fellowship with Him. He created man to worship Him.

He created you to be phenomenal, to do phenomenal things and to have a phenomenal life. You were born to win, designed for accomplishment, and engineered for success. After all, God don't make no junk! Everything God makes is phenomenal and that includes YOU!

In order to be the winner you were created to be, you must plan to win and prepare to win before you can expect to win. But when you plan to win and prepare to win, you can expect to win.

God created you for a specific purpose to solve a specific problem. That is your calling. God planted a dream in you that will make a difference in the world. You must awaken the dreamer within. Wake up! Pursue your purpose with passion!

Be grateful to God for everything and everyone in your life, including the thorns. There's a rose attached somewhere. We grow mostly through trials, so rejoice in them.

All of life is about relationships and relationships aren't always easy, but they are the most important thing in life and the only thing that will matter when you're gone. You *will* leave a legacy. You can choose what that legacy is by the way you treat others.

Create a vision for your life. Who will you become? What kind of spiritual life will you lead? What kind of thought life will you have? What kind of physical shape will you be in? What kind of family member will you be? What kind of work will you do? What kind of financial life will you have? What will your personal life be like?

Remember there are no impossibilities with God. God is Love and He has a phenomenal dream life planned for you. Therefore, in dreams and in love, there are no impossibilities. He is able to do exceedingly, abundantly above and beyond all you could ever think, ask or imagine, according to His power within you.

Remember that dreams do come true, so don't quit. The time will pass anyway, so you may as well invest that time going for it. Understand the process of dreaming. It's hard work! Be aware of how you are feeling, what you are thinking, and what is happening around you. Be willing to change. Face your fears with faith! Stay focused, implement, and be consistent. Eventually, you will become a different, better person if you follow the process. You will become the person you were created to be.

Create a picture in your mind of your preferred future and don't let go of it. You cannot go some place that you do not first see in your mind's eye. You have to conceive it before you can receive it or achieve it. Humans do what humans see.

A dream is an inspiring picture of the future that energizes your mind, your will, and your emotion, empowering you to do everything you can to achieve it. Your dream fuels your life. If you have the right dream, you'll be on fire. Ignite the passion that is waiting to be lit!

Remember, the dream starts with you. It starts inside of you with the inspiration that comes from a phenomenal vision. But remember, you must take action. So, go! Act! Implement. Go confidently. Go confidently in the direction of your dreams and you'll be met with unexpected success that is uncommon in common hours.

Dream intentionally. Set aside a time and a place where you can think, pray, dream and draw. Meditate on the Word of God and you'll be transformed by the renewing of your mind. The Truth will set you free.

Conclusion

When you experience fear, focus on facts. Faith equals freedom. Walking in the flesh equals fear. Feed your faith and you'll have freedom. Feed your flesh and you'll have fear.

Stay humble. Be grateful to God and don't take anything for granted. Be kind to others. Love them because they are phenomenal, too. Say good morning to God when you wake up and talk to Him throughout the day. He is your loving Father. Don't be anxious. Do not fear. In the world you'll have trouble, but He created the world and He has you in the palm of His hand. Rest in that.

Remember that He will supply your every need according to His riches in glory in Christ Jesus, and you can do all things through Him who strengthens you.

When you do all of this, you'll be at the top, and maybe even over the top.

I love you.

Your friend, Howard.

www.ingramcontent.com/pod-product-compliance
Lightning Source LLC
Chambersburg PA
CBHW022114090426
42743CB00008B/847